P9-DYJ-983

This Is How to Get Your Next Job

An Inside Look at What Employers Really Want

□ □ □ □ □ □ □ □ □ □ □ □ □ □ □ □

andrea kay

foreword by
richard n. bolles

AMACOM AMERICAN MANAGEMENT ASSOCIATION

New York · Atlanta · Brussels · Chicago · Mexico City
San Francisco · Shanghai · Tokyo · Toronto · Washington, D.C.

Bulk discounts available. For details visit:
www.amacombooks.org/go/specialsales
Or contact special sales:
Phone: 800-250-5308
E-mail: specialsls@amanet.org
View all the AMACOM titles at: www.amacombooks.org
American Management Association: www.amanet.org

This publication is designed to provide accurate and authoritative information in regard to the subject matter covered. It is sold with the understanding that the publisher is not engaged in rendering legal, accounting, or other professional service. If legal advice or other expert assistance is required, the services of a competent professional person should be sought.

Library of Congress Cataloging-in-Publication Data

Kay, Andrea, 1954-
  This is how to get your next job : an inside look at what employers really want / Andrea Kay; foreword by Richard N. Bolles.
    pages cm
  Includes index.
  ISBN 978-0-8144-3221-1 (pbk.) -- ISBN 0-8144-3221-2 (pbk.) 1. Job hunting. 2. Employment interviewing. 3. Career development. I. Title.
  HF5382.7.K39 2013
  650.14--dc23
                                  2012051814

Portions of this work were previously published in slightly different form in the author's syndicated columns.

© 2013 Andrea Kay
All rights reserved.
Printed in the United States of America.

This publication may not be reproduced, stored in a retrieval system, or transmitted in whole or in part, in any form or by any means, electronic, mechanical, photocopying, recording, or otherwise, without the prior written permission of AMACOM, a division of American Management Association, 1601 Broadway, New York, NY 10019.
  The scanning, uploading, or distribution of this book via the Internet or any other means without the express permission of the publisher is illegal and punishable by law. Please purchase only authorized electronic editions of this work and do not participate in or encourage piracy of copyrighted materials, electronically or otherwise. Your support of the author's rights is appreciated.

About AMA
American Management Association (www.amanet.org) is a world leader in talent development, advancing the skills of individuals to drive business success. Our mission is to support the goals of individuals and organizations through a complete range of products and services, including classroom and virtual seminars, webcasts, webinars, podcasts, conferences, corporate and government solutions, business books, and research. AMA's approach to improving performance combines experiential learning—learning through doing—with opportunities for ongoing professional growth at every step of one's career journey.

Printing number

ACC LIBRARY SERVICES AUSTIN, TX

In memory of my father, who gave me my first job when I was five and taught me how to be the best pencil sharpener the world would ever know. And in honor of my mother, who has supported me in everything I've ever done.

DISCARD

DISCARD

contents

foreword

If you are looking for a job, I recommend you read this book. But before we talk about *why*, I want you to think about what a strange practice this is: One author recommending the books of another author. It happens all the time. Why do authors recommend other authors, particularly those writing in the same field? You don't find that happening in other arenas of the marketplace. Does Coca-Cola recommend Pepsi? Nope, it does not. In commerce, you don't recommend a competitor's product. And why? There is a simple rule operating here: Consumers only have a finite amount of money. If they spend it on a competing product, they have less to spend on you. Therefore, isn't it mildly insane for authors to recommend that people spend their money on other authors' books, rather than their own? Well, I can really only speak from my own experience. But for me it makes perfect sense. For three reasons.

First, *overwhelm*. The Book of Ecclesiastes, in the Old Testament, enunciated the problem: *"Be warned, my son. . . . Of the making many books, there is no end. . . ."* To illustrate this sentence, as of August 2010, according to Google, there were 129,864,880 books in existence. Now, I have no idea how many of these books are in the careers or job-hunting field, but after writing in this field for literally decades, I can tell you it is a mind-boggling number. You want to read something? You want to read something *helpful?* One hardly knows where to begin. There are so many choices. I like to help by calling attention to those books—this one in particular—that stand out above the rest of the crowd.

Second, *voice.* I am the author of a book that has sold over 10 million copies and has for 40 years been the best-selling job-hunting book in the world. But, as with all books, there are a number of people who cannot hear my voice. The reasons don't matter. They just can't. They need another voice, even if it is conveying basically the same message, a voice that speaks to their heart, as mine does not and never will. Andrea's book speaks truths that I have emphasized for years, but here they are in a different voice. A lovely and knowledgeable voice. What truths, you ask? That *you have to enter into the world and the mind of employers, if you are job hunting.* That *you have to have found out as much as you can about a company or organization before you go to interview there.* That *job interviews are more like dating than they are like selling a used car.* That *you, as much as the employer, are trying to use the job interview to gather information, and then make a decision.* That *self-knowledge precedes market knowledge, in priority and importance.* If you are hunting for new work or a new career, it is crucial to know these things. And to choose the voice that will help you hear them best.

And, finally, *depth.* Andrea writes about the job interview with far greater depth than I did in my book—or most other books on this subject. She writes with authority. She has interviewed countless employers and asked them a question I never asked: Why *didn't* you hire the last ten people you interviewed? Out of their answers, Andrea has constructed a thoughtful, effective series of strategies that will benefit every job hunter who reads this book. I think this kind of depth was always needed on the subject of the job interview, but now more so than ever, in today's tough economy. This book is a gift. So, buy it. Read it. Use it. *Please.*

Richard N. Bolles, author
What Color Is Your Parachute?
A Practical Manual for Job-Hunters and Career-Changers
2013 edition; rewritten annually

Introduction

□ □ □ □ □ □ □ □ □ □

Why I Had to Write
This Book

THERE WERE TWO REASONS.

Reason #1: I couldn't stand listening to myself yell at the radio any longer.

I don't know about you, but I hate listening to myself yell—no matter what. But particularly when I'm alone and the point I'm yelling about will not make a lick of difference since no one but my dog and two cats can hear it.

In this case, I was getting ready for the day. Across the room I could hear the radio with a news report about jobs and unemployment.

An unemployed woman in Kansas was talking about how she sent out her resume with the same cover letter to 150 employers. "And I didn't get a single response," she exclaimed.

"Don't do that!" I yelled.

The interviewer asked a man in Florida what kind of work he'd like to do. He replied, "I'm looking for something where I can use my skills with people and maybe with computers."

"Don't say that!" I shouted.

When asked what she wanted, a young woman who had been trying to get work for a year said, "Well, ya know, I'm like a, well, I wanna be like a English and communications major. But I can't find a job in it."

Yes, I yelled again: "Don't do that!"

Reason #2: I wanted to know if my husband was crazy.

For more than six months I had watched him try to find an employee for his small business. He'd come home complaining about what potential employees were saying and doing in e-mails and during interviews he'd held at Starbucks, over lunch, in his office, and by phone.

Then one night he said, "That's it. End of story. No more. I give up." He was genuinely sad and discouraged about the whole thing.

Was it him? Was he right? I started talking to employers at small, medium, and large companies to find out. All over the country, they were experiencing the same thing. They had job openings, but said they couldn't find good people to fill them. They also told me what candidates were doing that led them to that conclusion. Turns out there was a complete mismatch of priorities and expectations.

If only workers could hear this. With the job market thick with fear and so much desperation among workers and misunderstanding between them and employers, I thought, *perhaps I could bridge the gap a bit.*

Most job hunters tell me their goal is to "stand out" to get noticed and hired—and how hard that is. Employers agree it's important to stand out. But, they say, it's not that hard. It's a matter of *not* doing what everybody else is doing.

Before you delve into those specifics, which are in my "don't do that/do this" advice (Chapters 3 through 6), it's key that you read Chapters 1 and 2. Because to apply the Don'ts and Do's effectively, you'll need to understand:

- How employers think *today*

- How to stand out among the millions you're competing with

- Why employers may not be hiring you

- What employers are looking for and why they'd hire you

- How you want to come across to employers

- How to show employers who you really are

- How to show employers you've got the skills the job calls for and are the type of person they want

- How to reinforce the impression you want to make before, during, and after an interview

That and more is what I cover in the first two chapters and will refer back to again and again in later chapters.

The Don'ts and Do's I share apply to anyone who sets out to find employment today. You could be looking for your first job, be a seasoned worker, be going for a completely new career, or be looking for contract work. The things you should never do, say, or wear have been done, said, and worn by 25-year-olds as well as senior executives.

How did I come up with the specific "Don'ts"? Mostly from the employers I talked to who had jobs to fill in the east, the south, or the middle parts of the United States, out west, in Canada, and in other places in the world.

I also looked at what my clients and readers were doing and say-ing and what I saw getting in their way of being hired—especially today. I listened to the parents of new college graduates who told me what their kids were doing. Many people don't even realize that what they're doing is making the difference between rejection and a job offer.

There is no question that looking for work can be daunting. It's a bit like hitchhiking, which I wouldn't recommend these days. After an hour of cars and trucks whizzing by, desperation kicks in. You wonder, "Will anyone ever stop and pick me up? Or will I be here, standing on the side of this road, forever?"

It may be hard to fathom at this moment, but you will not be standing in this place forever. In time, you will get noticed, appreci-ated, and hired by the right employer. This book will show you how to make that moment happen a whole lot sooner.

one

□ □ □ □ □ □ □ □ □ □

You Are What You Seem

Everyone's got an opinion. You do. My mother certainly does—especcially about my hair, shoes, and clutter in my closets. But that's another matter and nothing you need to concern yourself with.

The opinions you should be attentive to are those held by the big "They"—the people who can hire you.

These are people like Eric Zuckerman, Rob Basso, Michael Zwick, Dianne Durkin, Sander Daniels, Allan Young, and Alex Churchill, all successful business owners. These folks—plus plenty more like them—have jobs they're trying to fill. Jobs? Yes. There are jobs begging to be filled.

Maybe they have the perfect one for you. Maybe not. Later, you'll hear more about them and other hiring managers hungry for the right people to work at their companies. For now, you'll want to hear what they and others who hire people for their organizations think, and *why*. Because understanding that will help you stand out among millions of other workers competing for the same jobs and will be your ticket to getting hired today and in the future.

Of course they don't represent every employer. But what they think overall is pretty much what every employer I've talked to—from small to medium and large companies in all types of industries—has told me. You don't have to talk to every employer to know this: *When it comes to finding good people, it's really, really, really hard.*

It's so hard, some employers have given up looking.

How can that be? With millions of able-bodied unemployed or unhappily employed workers, why can't they find people to hire? What do they want that they're not finding?

It's not what you'd assume—the right technical or functional skills—or what most people call "the right skills."

And it's not the right experience either.

Yes, experience and skill matter . . .

And yes, some jobs in information technology, finance, engineering, and other areas are hard to fill because special talents and functional skills are needed to perform the jobs. At a time when everyone (politicians, employers, headhunters, recruiters, and futurists) is obsessed with talking about jobs, many also point to skill and talent shortages. In *some* areas.

And yes, for many jobs, education can also be a factor.

But . . .

For now, assume you have the so-called "right" experience, technical skills, or education. Because, as you'll hear in a moment, even with all of that, employers say they still can't find the right people.

You may be the most talented person who ever walked the good earth and possess the right and proper technical skills. But you still may not get hired. Here's why: it's *how you seem.*

Why They Aren't Hiring You

I asked employers this simple question: Why didn't you hire the last 10 people you interviewed? And you know what every one of them said? It was because of how the job applicant *seemed* based on how he or she *acted*. Before, during, or after an interview. Sometimes it was what a person did or didn't do, or said or didn't say. In an e-mail. On the phone. Or face-to-face. It could happen in the first three minutes of an interview. Or as one manager told me, in the last three minutes of walking an interviewee toward the exit.

Fair or not, the employers said the behaviors people exhibited were very revealing. The behavior influenced them so much that it predicted not only what kind of employee someone might be and whether the person could do the job, but also that elusive, hard-to-nail-down issue: whether the person would be a "good fit" at their company. Turns out most people didn't "fit," according to the employers. More on "fit" later.

" There's a correlation between the response you send an employer and how someone would be on the job. It is predictive of someone's performance."
—The conclusion of Bill Strauss, chairman of Strauss & Troy, a Cincinnati law firm, after trying to find a part-time marketing director

I should point out that these employers didn't come to this conclusion lightly. It took months—even a year—of interviewing candidates for the open positions they had that led them to feel discouraged and disheartened about finding good people for their organizations. As one CEO of a small East Coast business told me after dozens and dozens of interviews, "We all know there is massive unemployment. What I want to know is, where are the qualified, hardworking employees?"

So according to employers eager to hire and build their businesses, whether to hire or not hire someone—or even bring them in for an interview—came down to this: how the job applicant *seemed.*

Now before you have a conniption, thinking: *What can I do about that? I don't control how employers think about me and how I seem to them!* hear me—and them—out.

Naturally you don't control their brains. How someone feels about you when they first meet you depends on many things. According to Jack Mayer, professor of psychology at the University of New Hampshire, factors that can influence how someone feels about you include a person's frame of mind at a particular moment. The temperature outside. Whether you're similar to that person and whether you make the person feel appreciated. Personal beliefs, preconceptions, and experiences will factor in.

And sometimes you can't do a darn thing about meeting someone's criteria. Mayer, who once helped a car dealership with hiring, told me that the sales manager said the only criterion he used when deciding whether to hire someone was the applicant's astrological sign.

But that's a whole other issue.

When it comes to people deciding how they *feel* about you, the process is not straightforward and perfectly logical. They don't analyze what they see, but "we do react to how we feel when we see it . . . and after a few moments, we have formulated a conclusion," according to Kenneth Manges, forensic psychologist.

Since employers are human, they also do what psychologists call "negative filtering"—focusing on the negative and failing to pay attention to the positive, according to psychologist Elizabeth Lombardo.

"The human mind is a mismatch detector, always noticing what's wrong before it notices what's right," explains sociologist BJ Gallagher. "Our brains are hardwired to notice what's missing, out of place, or faulty."

So guess what happens? There's a tendency to see one less-than-perfect trait and overgeneralize that you're not the right fit, says Lombardo.

But you still have more power than you think to influence what they conclude about you: by what you say and do. And I'm going to share with you what you can *stop* doing and saying, and *start* doing and saying so that they stay interested. These are things you *do* control. For now, let's focus on how *they* think and what's behind it.

Their thinking may seem picky. But when you hear it from their side, it's not so unreasonable. In fact, if you were in their shoes, you'd probably think and feel the same way. We'll test that later.

Even in a good economy, getting hired or not comes down to whether you can do the job and what kind of employee you seem to be. Even in prosperous, thriving times, people with the power to hire are deciding who you are by how you *seem*—based on how you *act*.

But in a tenuous economy—when employers don't have the luxury, time, or money to make costly hiring mistakes—they put even more emphasis on how you *are* and how you *seem* to them, and whether to hire you as a result. In difficult economic times, there is less leeway and less tendency to give someone the benefit of the doubt when it comes to hiring. Employers will be more watchful of what you say and do. And they should be.

They've Been Burned

Some have become cynical and wary because of bad experiences with new hires in recent years. These were people given the benefit of the doubt. People in whom the employers had faith. People they wanted to believe could do the job.

Take the time Dianne Durkin, president of Loyalty Factor, a consulting and training firm in Portsmouth, New Hampshire, hired a new person after months of interviews. The night before the employee was to start, Durkin got an e-mail from the person saying, "I decided not to take the job," with no explanation.

The next person she hired (who had been out of work for two years) came into her office his second day and said, "Boy, you guys really work hard. I don't think I can do this," and left.

So now when she interviews, she watches for signs that someone is unprofessional and unreliable. One simple test: Do they follow up as they say they will?

To test this and determine whether someone is right for the company she gives assessment tests. But it's not just the answers to the test she looks at. It's *how* the person handles it.

In one instance, she gave an applicant the test to take home with the agreement that the person would send the results the next morning.

"The applicant calls later that morning saying she just woke up," explains Durkin. "She sounded very confused, saying she just had a big argument with her husband. I think she was drunk or on drugs, she was so incoherent. She called back three or four times, saying, 'I really need this job.'"

Then there was the person who might have had the right skill set, but wanted to be paid under the table. Can you blame her for thinking the applicant was dishonest?

An entrepreneur in Ohio spent nearly $30,000 to prepare his office and train his first employee. He had interviewed about 75 people over six months before he hired a young woman just two years out of college. After four-and-a-half months on the job his new employee, who never mentioned being unhappy, drove to the office in the middle of the night, packed up her things, and e-mailed her resignation.

Durkin, who consults with other small businesses, says, "I hear daily from hiring managers saying they cannot find competent professional candidates who have a solid work ethic, dress properly, and have good communications skills. They ask me, when hiring, how do you read between the lines to determine real competence vs. fluff?"

One way employers do that is to pay close attention to what job hunters say and do, and how that matches up with what they're looking for. Here, more specifically, is what they have concluded about the hundreds of job hunters they've encountered, how the employers came to those conclusions, and what led them to say, "Sorry, we're not interested."

Bad Behavior Is Making the Rounds

WHAT WERE YOU THINKING?

When an applicant shared vivid details about her personal problems in an interview, warning bells went off for Eric Zuckerman, president of PacTeam Group, a global manufacturer of custom-designed displays, packaging, and fixtures in Paramus, New Jersey, and around the world.

"For twenty minutes she's going on about how this happened and then that happened and how she got really depressed. Then she went to see a doctor."

What did he conclude? Her behavior showed poor judgment and lack of professionalism.

Another time he was interviewing a woman who seemed to have some skills the project management role needed—good design sense and creativity. The applicant left him a DVD with her portfolio to review after the interview.

"I go home and I'm sitting there with my wife, pop in the DVD and it's a bunch of artistic nude poses of her [the interviewee]. Then there's a video of her interviewing a naked couple who are in bed with each other."

Now come on, you can't help but wonder: What was she thinking? Wouldn't this incident lead any sensible person to question the kind of judgment she'd display on the job?

Here's a less dramatic example of poor judgment that ruined an applicant's chances for an offer. This incident took place at Thumbtack.com, a San Francisco–based firm that directs people to services in their cities. The CEO, along with the co-founder and director of user happiness, Sander Daniels, was holding a lengthy interview.

"We took a short break to eat a little dinner," explains Daniels. "Our CEO, being friendly, said we have soda and seltzer and jokingly mentioned that the candidate could have a beer. And he did. He proceeded to finish the beer while our chief engineer interviewed him.

"He was a younger person and it didn't occur to him that drinking a beer during an interview wasn't a great idea. He didn't make the cut."

The guy was no slouch. But when it came to showing good judgment this was not a slick move.

YOU SURE ARE TOUCHY

Daniels got insight into another applicant who initially did well when asked complicated technical questions. But then he "broke down when we pushed him on technical areas with which he wasn't familiar." He gave vague answers and when asked for details "became exasperated and said, 'Look, I don't know as much about hardware—my answers to the other questions were good, though!'"

This reaction signaled that on the job he "will take criticism personally," says Daniels.

A promising candidate who interviewed at ShelfGenie Franchise Systems, a company based in Marietta, Georgia, that designs, builds, and installs customized shelving, looked great on paper, but in person "was immature, very erratic, not focused, all over the map," says CEO Allan Young. Did the candidate have the ability to be creative? Yes. But he "seemed like he would be difficult to manage and wouldn't be receptive to direction or constructive criticism," says Young.

Notice the words he uses: the person "seemed like . . . "

ALL YOU WANT IS A "JOB" OR PAYCHECK

An owner of a medium-size company who had been looking for someone he could groom to eventually take over his business had one key requirement: the person had to want a *career*, not just a job at his company.

"I want people who understand what we're doing and want to be a part of that. All I get are responses that indicate they are merely looking for a job and a paycheck."

Like this one: In his first correspondence with the company, an applicant sent a PowerPoint presentation that included his requirement for an office and car allowance. Or like the person who sent her resume with this note: "I saw you were looking for someone. If this is what you are looking for, let me know."

"I don't know if the people who respond that way are just desperate or stupid. Either way, I'm not interested," the business owner said. And that pretty much sums it up.

CAN'T YOU JUST FOLLOW DIRECTIONS?

Rob Basso, who owns Advantage Payroll Services, which provides payroll, tax filing, and human resource services in Freeport, New York, looks for people who have the ability to write well. But following directions is also important. When his company posted a job opening, it specifically asked for a writing sample. Out of more than 100 responses, he didn't get a single sample.

Based on these responses, Basso certainly doesn't know if the applicants have the writing skills he needs. But it doesn't take a genius to conclude that these respondents don't follow directions well. It stands to reason that the way these people *act* makes an employer wary about whether they'd be that way on the job.

HELLO? DO YOU REALLY WANT THIS JOB?

Job offers have gone down the toilet when Zuckerman invites someone back for a second interview but doesn't hear back for a week or two. The excuses pour in: My computer was down. I had a funeral, an operation, a family emergency, a sick child. I was out of the country.

"I'm not insensitive, but it's so easy to communicate in this day and age. I can only assume someone's not interested," he says.

Lack of responsiveness and other lackadaisical behavior also make the employer wonder: Will the applicant be that way on the job?

An entrepreneur with a growing business in a competitive environment says there is no margin for error when it comes to hiring. In his quest to find just the right employee, he was encouraged when he met a young man who seemed to have what he needed. He gave the young man his card and said, "Call me."

"He had critical thinking skills and got an A in his writing class. He said he'd e-mail me the next day."

A week later, the employer got an e-mail that in so many words said, "Sorry I didn't get back to you, something came up."

His weak and week-late response told the employer he wasn't the right one.

"To hire someone with little or no experience I have to invest a lot of time and energy. It's a big leap. I kick butt in my work and associate with people who share that trait. His lax and late response told me he wasn't that interested. He lacked the drive and ambition that would warrant my investment."

The young man called a week later, insisting he had all of that. "OK, send me five writing samples," said the employer.

"Just out of school I knew he wouldn't have the kind of writing I need. Maybe, though, I'll see that spark."

Unfortunately, not only was there no spark but there were also enough typographical errors to reinforce the employer's first impression.

The young man sent an e-mail asking if the employer had read his samples. Feeling as if he could at least offer advice, the employer spent another hour giving a writing critique. The young man apologized for the typographical errors, saying he had dropped what he was doing to immediately send the samples and had sent his rough draft files, adding it had slipped his mind that the correct files were on a different computer.

The employer told him: "In a professional environment like mine, if I don't deliver work that's not 100 percent professional and buttoned down, I lose my house."

The young man was offended by being judged, insisting he was up for the task.

"Yes, I'm judging you," explained the employer.

It's a cold fact of the job hunter's life: "I don't judge people on their intentions. People are judged by their actions. You haven't even checked out my website to know what I do. You send me work with typos. You respond with an excuse."

If only, says the employer, "he had been as passionate about his interest in my company and this opportunity as he was in defending his actions."

Companies that have difficulty recruiting reported gaps in job applicants in four areas: critical thinking and problem solving, professionalism and work ethic, written communications, and leadership, according to a 2011 survey of more than 2,280 human resource professionals in eight industries conducted by Society for Human Resource Management.

**AT LEAST DEMONSTRATE THE SKILLS
YOU WANT TO GET PAID FOR**

The president of a prestigious business who had been advertising for a salesperson told me he got an e-mail that was so generic "it could have been written to Sam's Pawn Shop."

So he wrote the person back asking, "What do you know about us?"

"Not much," the applicant responded.

"This guy is applying for a position in which he'd get new clients. This job is based on understanding those clients and what they do. If he's not willing to do that for a potential employer, how does he have the skills to do it for our company? It's not that hard to do a half an hour of research to learn what the organization is up to and then tailor your communication."

He adds: "People send passionless, desperate inquiries and think that having an interview with me will miraculously transform them into someone I'll want to hire. But they won't get the interview if they act this way in their initial contact."

Basso was interviewing a candidate for a customer service role who asked, "Do I need to have math skills? I'm not very good at math."

"How could you ask that question at a payroll company?" Basso says. "Did this person not know what payroll meant? It is a significant gaffe when you're up against 100 other people."

It's Worse Than Ever

Employers everywhere say they are more tuned in to these issues because today, more than ever, job hunters seem desperate and willing to say anything to get a job.

People oversell themselves and apply for jobs in which they have no background or experience. Zuckerman says he hears from mortgage brokers applying for designer jobs. "The mentality is that they think the more jobs they apply for, the odds are one will work out."

But the thinking is flawed. And it only puts employers in a bad mood and makes them skeptical of your motivation. (It's also a huge waste of your time.) I talk more about this in Chapter 3. Besides realizing that you're not qualified in the least (and, therefore, not able to give a good rationale for wanting the job), most employers will conclude you're not truly interested in the job—only in a paycheck until something in your field comes along.

"When we have an opening, it's not just a job for someone to do until they can get what they really want," points out Zuckerman.

And although technology has made it easier for people to apply for jobs, it has led them to be more careless.

People are in such a rush that they send employers like Zuckerman responses like this: "Here is my resume for consideration." That's it. And that's the norm, he says.

> **"** It's often the little things that are telling of bigger problems."
> —Michael Zwick, president of Assets International, a private investigation
> agency that locates missing heirs and beneficiaries

HERE'S WHAT'S GOING ON IN THE EMPLOYER'S MIND
If you act like this now, you'll act like this on the job.
Employers are watching and listening before, during, and after an interview, all the while thinking:

- If you're careless with your correspondence and follow-up, you'll be careless with the work you do for me.

- If you act immature and unprofessional, you'll be that way on the job here.

- If you aren't reliable about showing up and following up in the interview process, you won't be reliable at your job here.

◻ If you get annoyed and short with interview questions or the process, you'll be difficult to deal with on the job.

◻ If you show poor judgment now, you'll handle our customers, clients, and others the same way.

◻ If you can't sell me, how will you sell my customers?

◻ If you don't follow up and are full of excuses, you'll be full of excuses about why your work isn't done.

Can't You Just Be More Like This?

Later we'll talk in more detail about how to show an employer the great work you can do for the company. You'll learn more specifically about what employers can't help notice, what they would like to see, and how they know it when they see it—based on what you do and say.

For now, here is a list of the broader categories of what employers want. Consciously or not, fair or not, they're judging you on your actions (not your intentions) based on what you say and do. Here's what employers are looking for:

What Employers Look For

1. Consistent, stable behavior
2. Clear, critical thinking
3. Maturity
4. Professionalism
5. Excitement about the job and the industry
6. Positive, can-do attitude
7. Self-initiative
8. Inventive, innovative, creative thinking

9. *Desire to grow with the company*

10. *Intellectual curiosity*

11. *Eagerness to learn and excel*

12. *Ability to work well with others and on teams*

13. *Flexibility and adaptability*

14. *Gumption and passion that says you're worth the investment it will take to train you*

15. *Desire to be a part of something bigger than yourself*

16. *Ability to communicate*

17. *Leadership potential and that "special something"*

As you can see, this isn't a checklist pertaining to experience or functional skills. These are behaviors, qualities, characteristics, sensibilities, attitudes, and demeanor. Employers don't have the time or money to hire the wrong people. They know which attitudes and characteristics work well and which don't. And they are watching and listening for signs of which ones you have.

Someone (I'd tell you who it was if I knew) said that companies hire for skills and fire for character. What these employers and others are saying is that they indeed also hire for character.

❝ *Imagination is more important than knowledge."*
—Albert Einstein

This seems like a good place to remind you of what I said earlier: Yes, some jobs require a particular level of expertise, knowledge, and functional skill. Even if you're just out of school, a certain level of proficiency in your subject matter is expected (although no one expects you to know everything).

Points are definitely given for having expertise and a certain set of skills. So, please hear me when I say this: It isn't that technical skills don't matter. They do.

As the economy in the United States has picked up and emerging markets around the world grow, companies of all sizes need workers with particular skills to meet the demand.

At the 2012 World Economic Forum Annual Meeting in Davos, Switzerland, Manpower Group published a paper, titled "Increasing Demand for Better Skills Assessment and Match for Better Results," that said this well:

> "Converging macro-economic forces and demographic shifts mean skilled individuals are in short supply" and "under-qualified workers remain abundant."

To some employers, technical skills can matter more than anything—until the rest matters more.

I remember one company I consulted with that had a so-called "genius" software engineer who had risen to the ranks of upper management. He was a jerk: rude, insensitive, and arrogant. Everyone—including clients—hated him. His staff even quit.

Why would the company keep him? He was really smart when it came to developing the company's product. Plus—and this is probably the biggest reason—his boss (who had an ego the size of Lake Erie) had recruited him from a competitor and refused to see how he poisoned the business. Finally, when the company lost two major clients, the software engineer was fired. This is an example of hiring for skills and firing for character.

These days most companies can't afford to keep someone like that. They're watching closely for cues. They're hiring for character plus technical skills.

Of course many jobs—astrophysicists, CPAs, even cowboys—

require specialized skills. But who would you rather hire: a cowboy who had the right skills and knowledge—like handling animals and repairing and maintaining equipment and buildings—who seemed like a lazy, grumpy son-of-a-gun? Or a cowboy with the right skills and knowledge who also had initiative and a positive, can-do attitude?

And if you were in the market for an astrophysicist at your university, who would you rather hire: an astrophysicist with the necessary skills to analyze and research but who hated talking to live humans? Or an astrophysicist with the necessary skills who enjoyed the company of his colleagues and students?

"Experience can be overrated in hiring," says Joe Cheung, director of recruiting for Yammer, a growing software enterprise firm in San Francisco. "It's much more important to hire somebody who is going to be able to solve a problem in a new way and who is creative about decision making."

Given the choice between someone with experience in a given area and someone who appears to be a really good problem solver, David Sacks, CEO of Yammer, is willing to bet on the problem solver.

Even Google, which like any company wants to find the right combination of experience and personal characteristics, would pick the less-experienced person with the right attitude, a company spokesperson says. It's not just your coding skills they care about.

In its 2009 Interviewing Do's and Don'ts survey, the Society for Human Resource Management asked employers this question: If two job candidates with limited experience were applying for the same job at your company, what type of prior experience would tip the balance in one candidate's favor: (a) A paid job (even if it wasn't directly in the candidate's career field) that gave the person "real-world" work experience, or (b) An unpaid internship directly in the candidate's career field, showing that the candidate is willing to work hard to gain relevant experience?

Seventy percent of employers picked B—the option that said the candidate seemed to be "willing to work hard."

"If you're 25, it's not your experience I'm looking at," says Eric Zuckerman of PacTeam Group. "You don't have any. It's your intelligence, excitement, professionalism, attention to details, the fact that you're taking this seriously and you want to be part of our company that I care about."

A Job Offer from Steve Jobs

After about five dozen interviews over three months at NeXT (the company founded by Steve Jobs after he left Apple in 1985) Steve Jobs made BJ Gallagher an offer.

Gallagher, a sociologist and author, had been interviewing for the director of executive development job at NeXT. But in the last interview, Jobs offered her the director of recruitment role—a job she knew nothing about.

"I asked him, 'Why would you hire someone with no experience in this field?' and he said: 'I believe in getting good talent on board and we'll sort it out when we get it here.'"

If she didn't have the experience or knowledge to do the job, what did she have that he wanted so badly? Charisma. Enthusiasm. Passion.

This wasn't the first time that happened to her. Earlier in her career she applied for the director of training and organizational development job at the University of Southern California. She had experience in continuing education but none in this specific area. Even so, she got the job.

Later, the assistant vice president who hired her told her how he made his decision. He said he told his boss: "She didn't know shit about training, but she sure can light up a room"—and he had to hire her.

She also had a great love for the university and a lot of knowledge of how things worked on campus. By the end of the interview, she says, "He had fallen in love with my passion for learning" and more. Her boss taught her what she needed to learn. For the next three years, "We made a great team."

"GOOD FIT"

What is it and what are you trying to fit into?

It's hard to explain, and employers have a hard time describing it. But they know "fit" when they see it.

They're constantly monitoring for it in your e-mails, letters, and resume. They're on the alert when listening to you chat away on the phone and sitting across from you in person. They pick up clues from how you react to questions, how you conduct yourself and treat others—all things we've already talked about. We'll cover even more in later chapters.

Most likely they're not sitting there saying to themselves, "Now, I wonder if she is a proper fit?" Although some—which I'll show you in a minute—have developed an entire interview process based on the values that represent their culture.

To decipher whether or not you are a good fit, they are wondering, "What would it be like to have this person working at my company?"

Acting unfriendly or rarely smiling is one reason UserTesting. com, a service that tests a company website's usability, has decided someone wasn't a good fit, according to CEO Darrell Benatar. "We want to have a little fun working together too."

One thing an employer is deciding is whether you're likeable.

In his book *The Likeability Factor* Tim Sanders describes the four aspects of likeability as:

1. *Friendliness.* Do I feel good when meeting you? Do you make me feel welcome? Do you smile? Are you enthusiastic?

2. *Relevance.* How well do you connect to what I want or need? Do you share information that's relevant to me?

3. *Empathy.* Do you have a sense of what I may be going through or what motivates me?

4. *Being real.* Do you come off as genuine or are you busy trying to impress me?

You'll have a chance to influence all of these, as you'll learn in later chapters.

An Express Employment Professionals 2011 survey of over 17,000 clients across the United States and Canada found that half of the respondents believe it is "somewhat difficult to very difficult to recruit and fill positions." And it's not necessarily because of a lack of qualified people. "There is a huge volume of talented candidates on the market," Express says. "The best overall fit for the position and the company is the big challenge."

Seventy-nine percent of CFOs surveyed by Accountemps said an employee's sense of humor is important for fitting into a company's corporate culture, according to a poll of more than 1,400 executives conducted in January 2012.

VonChurch, a San Francisco–based firm that recruits workers for the digital entertainment industry, has a "values committee" that helps the company decide whether someone fits its culture. Made up of other employees, the committee asks questions that include "Did you enjoy the conversation with the person?" and "Was the person magnetic?"

The committee even utilizes a "values" booklet, which outlines the values the firm looks for in employees. According to the booklet, the purpose is to "keep VonChurch a fun place to work and full of innovation." These values are not just "words on brass plaques or cliché management expressions, but actual living guidelines for our company" when it comes to every decision, including hiring.

Humor is an important quality at VonChurch, says CEO Alex Churchill. "Recruitment work is 90 percent rejection," he says. So without a sense of humor, you'd have a tough time making it at his company.

Google looks for "Googliness," which is the company's way of describing cultural fit. If you're in an interview with Google, the interviewer is wondering, Is this someone I'd like to work with? Is this person an interesting addition to our team? Can this person thrive in a place that gives a lot of freedom?

In the company's early days it had what it called the "airport test." After an interview, the interviewers asked themselves, "If I were stuck with this person at the airport for two hours, would we have something interesting to talk about? Would I learn from this person?"

You don't work in a vacuum—you interact with others all day. So, Michael Zwick says that besides considering whether a person can do the job, he too looks at potential workers wondering, "Will this person mesh with the existing staff?"

Remember the woman who spilled the details of her personal problems to Eric Zuckerman? He concluded she was the wrong fit because she'd bring the wrong attitude.

"When you're going on about how the world has treated you so badly, I'm thinking, 'You've got Oscar the Grouch sitting here.' I want someone who's adding to our work experience and environment, and who brings positive energy."

Plus, to him, her behavior predicted how she would fit in with others. "I can only imagine what it would be like if she was working here. She seemed overly dramatic."

What are you fitting? The culture. The particular values that a company adheres to. The way things are done at the place. It can be hard to describe, but employers do know whether they see you fitting in or not.

> **"**I need to be able to visualize the person executing his or her job effectively and efficiently in harmony with the rest of the employees."
>
> —Hector Barresi, vice president of marketing
> and engineering for a multinational manufacturer

Is This Too Much to Ask For?

Think about those people you work with, or who work for you, who drive you nuts.

What is it that they do—or don't do?

Can't follow simple directions? Don't have a clue about how to tactfully handle customers, clients, coworkers, and senior management? Do they make it impossible to discuss problems or hear constructive feedback? Do they just show up and do the bare minimum, bitch and moan, blame everyone else, overreact to every little thing, not follow through? Do they rarely—if ever—take the lead?

This is exactly who employers don't want to hire. They're trying to decipher what kind of employee you'd be. The hope is to discover this from how you *seem* based on how you act before, during, and after interviews.

Imagine you owned a business or were responsible for hiring at your company. Wouldn't you be thinking along these lines? Go back to my What Employers Look For list. Would you be looking for those things? You bet.

Considering that, if you want to get hired, doesn't it make good sense to care about what "they" think?

- - - - - - - - - - - - - - - - - - -

"Would You Hire You?" Test

To take this test here's what you will need:

- A frame of mind that will help you be open-minded and honest with yourself

- A quiet place where you will not be interrupted

- A pen or pencil

- Something to write on

Think about the last five interviews you had and what you did before, during, and after. Write down your answers to these questions:

1. What did you do that showed you have good judgment?
   What did you do that may have demonstrated poor judgment?

2. How did you demonstrate that you are open to feedback, flexible, easy to work with, and eager to learn and excel?
   What did you do that may have signaled you take things personally or aren't receptive to feedback?

3. How did you indicate you are excited about being a part of the industry and the company and want to grow with it?
   Did you do anything that gave the impression you're desperate or only interested in a job or paycheck or until something better comes along?

4. What did you do that showed you follow direction well?

   What did you do that could make an employer think you don't follow direction?

5. *How did you convince the employer that you want the job beyond a shadow of a doubt?*
   What did you do that would give the impression you didn't care about the job and may lack drive and ambition?

6. *How did you prove through your correspondence, conversations, and follow-up that you have the necessary (or potential) skills for the job?*
   What did you do that would lead the employer to conclude you don't have the necessary (or potential) skills for the job?

7. *How did you demonstrate a positive, can-do attitude?*
   What did you do that may have made you seem negative?

8. *How did you show that you take initiative?*
   What did you do that gave the impression you don't think for yourself or aren't responsive?

9. *How did you show you are a creative, innovative thinker or problem solver?*
   What did you do that would make an employer think you don't have an innovative bone in your body?

10. *How did you help the employer see you work well with others?*
    What did you do that might make the employer question your likeability and ability to get along well with others?

11. *How did you show that you care about details and doing good, professional work?*
    What did you do that would make the employer question your commitment to do good, professional work?

12. *How did you demonstrate leadership potential or abilities?*
    What did you do that could lead the employer to conclude you are not leadership material?

13. *How did you reveal your passion about this opportunity and show you're worth the investment it will take to train you? What did you do that might lead the employer to think you're not serious, don't care enough, and are not worth their investment of time and money?*

14. *How did you prove you are a mature professional? What did you do that would make you seem immature or defensive?*

15. *How did you demonstrate clear, critical thinking? What did you do that might make you come across as a scatterbrained or ineffective communicator and thinker?*

The employer has to be able to "see" you fitting in with the business. Based on what you wrote, if you were an employer, would you hire you? Or would your behavior put doubts in your mind?

There Really Are Jobs Out There

I'm not even going to get into employment and unemployment statistics. Who knows how they will have changed between the time I've written this book and the time you're reading it. I will say this: The numbers will fluctuate.

But we do need to talk about this: what you tell yourself about the lack of or availability of jobs. Because that too can affect what you do and how you seem in the job-hunting process.

A lot of people go around saying, "There aren't any jobs" or "No one is hiring." News reports that dwell on the negative don't help. It's hard not to let it affect you. With those thoughts in your mind, you can act or seem desperate, careless, and impatient. And when you get nowhere after sending out 100 resumes, you may jump to the conclusion that there are no jobs.

But it just ain't so.

Millions of new jobs have been created in the last five years, and there are millions of open positions. Some are posted on job sites and company websites, or in professional publications. Others aren't publicized. Some only exist (for now) in the minds of business owners and teams of executives who are about to launch new products or services, fire someone, or start a new endeavor. They just haven't made it official.

Between late 2007—when the financial turmoil hit and all hell broke loose—and the time of this writing, plenty of businesses have had products and services to create and deliver, have been growing, and have needed to hire.

Opinions on where the jobs are and what will drive economic recovery vary. Some argue it's the small businesses and entrepreneurs who will move us forward. Others insist it's big businesses that employ thousands across the country and world.

But research conducted by The Ohio State University Fisher College of Business and General Electric Capital Corporation in 2011 says differently. It's actually the middle market doing the hiring, adding some two million jobs in recent years, according to the report "The Market That Moves America."

Middle market businesses have between $10 million and $1 billion in revenues per year. Who are they? They're all over the place—factories, construction companies, and professional services that vary in size, structure, and industry.

They are also all over the place in terms of ownership—publicly traded, privately owned, family owned, partnerships, and sole proprietorships. They tend to have a specialized niche. Some are in transition from being small businesses or start-ups to becoming bigger businesses.

There are approximately 200,000 of them, which is 3 percent

of all companies, contributing about 34 percent to private employment. That's about 41 million jobs.

These are the companies you notice when you're driving through a neighborhood you've never been. You see a place called Happy Chicken Farms and think, "I've never heard of them." (Happy Chicken Farms is a midsize family-owned business in Urbancrest, Ohio, that produces eggs and dairy products, serving small independent restaurants, supermarkets, schools, bakeries, and others. And it's been around since 1953.)

Or you might be heading through Orem, Utah, and see a building with an interesting round orange logo on the side and wonder, "What do they do?"

The company happens to be Fishbowl, a private, midsize company that makes inventory control software for QuickBooks users. Business is booming. Who knew?

Many such companies exist, but we don't hear a lot of references to the "middle market."

At the same time, temporary employment is up and manufacturing is rebounding. The auto industry is a good example. "Total jobs in all U.S. auto plants and parts factories will rise 10% to about 650,000 jobs this year, says the Center for Automotive Research, and hit 756,800 by 2015," said a *USA Today* article published on January 25, 2012.

There are some 600,000 skilled manufacturing jobs that are unfilled in the United States according to a 2011 survey titled "Boiling Point?" conducted by Deloitte Consulting LLP and the Manufacturing Institute. The survey of over 1,100 executives at manufacturing firms found that 67 percent of manufacturers have a moderate to severe shortage of qualified workers. And 56 percent anticipate the shortage to increase over the next three to five years. Recruiters say many people applying for these jobs are unqualified, and that besides the needed technical skills, they also lack essential cognitive skills—the ability to analyze, process, and understand new data and thoughts.

A Google official told me that the company, which employs 32,000 people, hired more workers in 2011 than in its entire history—more than 7,000 people.

Many of these jobs may not be for you. But you never can tell. Enough though, on that subject. This is not a book about *where* the jobs are. It's about how to get hired for the ones you discover that do fit you. There *are* jobs. And so, for the ones you potentially qualify for and have interviewed or applied for and have not gotten, the problem may lie in how you *seem* to the employers. And that's something you can fix.

> **❝** *I'm looking for somebody I want to talk to, somebody who is interesting, who wants to talk to me about some aspect of our company, some aspect of companies like ours . . . who I wish were working for me. When you see that, it's really pretty easy."*
>
> —Bill Kling, founder and president emeritus of the
> American Public Media Group, describing what he looks for when hiring
> (*New York Times*, January 15, 2012)

Making Peace with Where Things Are

You want to work. And employers need workers. To get hired you need, as Jack Mayer puts it, "to fit their preconceptions of whether you can do the job."

We don't know what every single employer's preconceptions will be. But we've covered broad categories of what employers want to see when they hire someone and insights into how they conclude whether you've got the goods.

Whether or not they "should" evaluate you based on how you

seem is fruitless to debate. So let's not. Employers are human and will go on acting like all humans: observing and judging how others seem based on what they see, experience, and sense. You will be judged by your actions, not your intentions. And that's the way it is. Like it or not.

The key to success in job hunting, and for that matter a less angst-ridden and more successful life in general, is to *start where things are*, not where you think they *should be*. This is where "they" are. They believe *you are what you seem*. If you want to get hired, you need to care about that.

Shall we move on now to what you can do about that?

two

□ □ □ □ □ □ □ □ □ □

Tell and Show

People tell me all the time that they "are" a certain way. But they sure don't act it.

"I'm focused. I'm a good communicator and I know exactly what I want," one young man told me when we met.

So I asked him: "What kind of job are you looking for?" To which he said: "I guess being in an office of some sort with a company."

Now you tell me. Does that sound like a focused, good communicator who knows exactly what he wants?

Yet he insisted over and over, "I really can communicate. I do know what I want."

I see resumes and e-mails that state these exact words: "I am a meticulous, thorough professional and pay close attention to details." The evidence says otherwise with typos and misspellings throughout the correspondence.

I hear job hunters describe themselves as strong, strategic communicators—the very essence of the job they want. Yet in an interview they can't even explain how they applied their strengths in previous jobs.

They insist, "But I really am a strategic thinker and communicator."

Sorry, I'm just not feeling it.

You are what you seem, as we discussed in Chapter 1. So the question is: *How do you want to seem?* And how will you convey that so it's more than just words? How will you actually ensure that you come across that way?

Before you contact the employers or go on another interview, you must, must, must (am I making myself clear?) answer these questions. Because if you can't precisely define how you want to seem and have *them* see you, they'll decide for you. Wouldn't you rather be the one to determine how that goes?

To make a positive impression and leave employers eager to hold a first interview, invite you back for a second interview, or hire you, you will need to not just *tell* them who you are, but also *show* them. *What you say about yourself must match up with how you actually are.*

The problem is that hardly anyone knows how to describe this. Could you? Can you explain right here and now how you want to *seem* to employers? I hear silence. If you don't know that, how can you show them? You won't.

It takes work to figure out the precise language that describes who you are and how you want to be seen. But everyone's been so busy thinking about the question they've heard a trillion times since they were wee tykes—"So what do you want to be when you grow up?"—they hardly ever consider what I'm about to ask you.

Unless you grew up with someone akin to George Washington, who went around saying things like, "I hope I shall always possess firmness and virtue enough to maintain what I consider the most enviable of all titles, the character of an honest man," it is doubtful you sit around and even think about this. It's a shame, really. Because this information can really pack a punch in a job hunt, not to mention a career.

But have no fear. You will get there. My exercises in this chapter will help you think this through. In this chapter you're going to delve into questions that will help you clarify what kind of person you want to be at work. What kind of character you want to display at the office. How you want others to feel in your presence. How you want to be thought of and what you want to be known for—personally and professionally.

This information will come in very handy in the next chapters. But for now, there is the matter of defining the admirable ways in which you want employers to see you, then tattooing this into your heart and mind.

Only then can you talk about—and then demonstrate and reinforce—those values, attitudes, and skills (and know when you're about to veer off course, which is particularly easy to do when you're under pressure). I don't care how quick you are on your feet; it's hard to keep it together when you're under the gun.

You may be detail-oriented and disciplined. But in a moment of stress, poof! There it goes. That fast.

Think about the young man in Chapter 1 who kept messing up throughout the pre-interview process. Remember, he sent the employer writing samples with typographical errors? The young man explained that he had dropped what he was doing to immediately send the samples and had shipped off his rough draft files. He came across as sloppy and unprofessional. He insisted *he wasn't like that* and was offended by being judged. But he sure was acting that way.

So first, we're going to get crystal clear on how you want to be seen.

The second exercise in this chapter will help you think through how you can *show* who you are. Because as I just explained to you through those examples, words are not enough. You must tell *and* show.

So these exercises will help you think through two issues:

1. How you want to *seem* to the employer.

2. What you'll *tell* prospective employers so they see you that way—and then *do* to show them you are actually that way, so it's not just talk.

Would-Be Employers Are Out to Reject You—And Fast

They don't mean to. They can't help themselves.

It's like shopping for jeans. When flipping through a three-foot high pile of denim, it only takes seconds to eliminate the unflattering styles or ones that simply don't work. Skinny jeans? No way. Double buttons at the top? Too much work to get in and out of. Back pockets with buttons? Who needs more layers? Low rise? Hate that gappy thing that happens when you sit. So now that you've found and eliminated the ones that have something wrong with them, it will be much easier to sort through what's left, right?

Employers' minds work much the same way. They're looking for "something wrong with you" so they can eliminate you, make their job easier, and be as efficient as possible in the process.

They are only human. They do what humans do—focus on the negative. In psychological terms, that's called "negative filtering."

Plus, they get a lot of resumes. According to Bersin & Associates Talent Acquisition Factbook 2011, companies receive 144 applications *on average for each entry-level or hourly opening and 89 applications on average for each professional-level job opening.*

So if they're deciding whether to meet you based on your resume, you don't get much of their attention before they conclude that you're in or you're out.

In fact, a 2011 CareerBuilder survey found that 72 percent of human resource managers spend less than two minutes reviewing an application, and 55 percent of hiring managers spend less than two minutes looking at an application.

An employer may not consciously be looking to eliminate you—especially that quickly—but will have the tendency to see one less-than-perfect trait and decide you're history.

You have the opportunity to *tell and show* at these three crucial times:

1. Before an interview—when you first contact an employer or follow up on an inquiry

2. During an interview—when you sit across the desk of your would-be boss or a hiring manager

3. After an interview—when you follow up

And don't forget, you're also creating and reinforcing "how you are" throughout your broader presence in social media and what you say on blogs and in other places on the Internet. We'll discuss this more in Chapter 3.

So, just how do you want to seem? Let's figure that out so "they" don't decide for you.

The "How You'll Be Remembered After You've Left the Room" Principle

You may recall the 2011 Academy Awards when actress Melissa Leo, upon being named best supporting actress, came up to the stage and began yammering: "Oh my, oh my God. Oh wow really, really really, really, really truly wow . . . OK. Yeah, I am kind of speechless. Golly sakes . . . " Then she used the "F" word.

I think she's a wonderful actress. But she's not exactly a household name. And after that exhibition, I fear that Leo's performance will lead her to be remembered mostly as the actress who blurted out a profanity at the Oscars.

That's how the "How You'll Be Remembered After You Leave the Room" Principle works. These things stick in people's minds.

Laura Orsini, an editor and writer in Phoenix, told me of the time she was listening to a speaker at a businesswomen's meeting who described herself as a "business pimp." The speaker went on to qualify the comment saying, "Of course, I'd never use that description for a roomful of bankers." Which got Orsini wondering: "Why in the world was it then OK for her to use the term when speaking to a collection of businesswomen? *Pimp* is an ugly word . . . usually a male who denigrates women . . . to make money. I could have done business with her, but chose not to follow up, as well as telling quite a number of people about the incident, all of who seemed equally repelled."

Was she overreacting? It doesn't matter. Damage done.

She says she never forgot this woman and the incident. Unfortunately for the speaker, it is not a positive memory. And she won't get much future business from that crowd.

Just remember this: The way *you'll* be remembered after you leave the room doesn't have to be negative. It all depends on *how you are*.

"How I Want to Be Remembered After I Leave the Room" Exercise

Here's what you will need:

- A nice cup of tea

- Your favorite pen or pencil

- Some paper

- This book—open to the next pages

- A quiet place away from your electronic doodads

- Enough quiet time to let yourself think, write, and focus

Complete the following questions. Some may overlap and elicit similar language. That's fine. Just write away.

WHEN I THINK ABOUT MY WORK AND CAREER AND HOW I OPERATE IN A WORKPLACE:

1. What specific qualities do I want to exhibit?

For example, I want to be seen as:

❑ Mature

❑ Professional

❑ Passionate about the work

❑ Positive

❑ Adventurousness

❑ Self-motivated

❑ A quick learner

❑ Creative

❑ Imaginative

❑ Honest

❑ Having high integrity

❑ Courageous

❑ Disciplined

❑ Determined

❑ Persistent

❑ Innovative

❑ Eager to learn

❑ Easy to talk to

❑ Open-minded

❑ Take charge

❑ Flexible

❑ Eager to excel

❑ Cooperative

❑ Detail-oriented

❑ Intuitive

❑ Humble

❑ Polite

❑ Competitive

❑ Team-oriented

❑ Empathetic

❑ Resourceful

❑ Budget-oriented

❑ Deadline-oriented

❑ Results-oriented

❑ Conscientious

❑ Responsive

❑ Charismatic

❑ Quick on my feet

❑ On the cutting edge

❑ Funny

❑ A big-picture thinker

❑ Conceptual yet practical

2. What beliefs and attitudes do I want to convey? What do I stand for? What are my guiding principles? What's my motto?

Samples:

❑ My work is an extension of who I am.

❑ I'm totally responsible for building my value and getting where I want to go.

❑ Relationships are the most important ingredient in my career.

❑ Quality, quality, quality.

❑ The buck stops here.

❑ You can count on me to get the job done.

❑ I love how technology is constantly changing.

❑ I am passionate about animation.

❑ I practice what I preach.

❑ I learn from making mistakes.

❑ I always do what I say I will do.

❑ The customer is always right.

❑ Innovation is the most important way to grow a business.

❑ I respond to every call and e-mail in a timely manner.

❑ It's not what you say but how you say it.

❑ I want to help my company be profitable.

❑ I am the ambassador for my employer.

❑ I am a problem solver.

❑ I want to have fun at work.

❑ I welcome criticism.

❑ I underpromise and overdeliver.

❑ I want to improve the lives of others.

❑ I want to make a difference through my work.

❑ I work hard and play hard.

3. How do I want others to feel in my presence?

Samples:

- ❑ Respected

- ❑ Understood

- ❑ Motivated

- ❑ Inspired

- ❑ Empowered

- ❑ Listened to

- ❑ Clear about my motivation and directions

- ❑ Valued

- ❑ An important part of the team

- ❑ Like it's OK to make a mistake

4. How do I want to approach problems, people, and opportunities?

Samples:

- ❑ With sensitivity to others

- ❑ With political savvy

- ❑ With enthusiasm

- ❑ With intellectual curiosity

- ❑ With an analytical eye

- ❑ With caution

- ❑ With openness

❑ With fairness

❑ With humility

❑ With confidence

❑ With good manners

WHEN I THINK ABOUT THE ACTUAL WORK I DO:

1. What are my top skills (strengths) and talents that I bring to an employer?
These are verbs—things you actually do. You enjoy doing them
and do these better than anything else—that's what makes them
strengths.

Samples include the ability to:

❑ Write

❑ Communicate concisely

❑ Lead others

❑ Analyze

❑ Research

❑ Methodically solve problems

❑ Build trusting relationships

❑ Train

❑ Present

❑ Conceptualize and translate concepts

❑ Write code

❑ Fabricate costumes and props

❏ Teach

❏ Organize and plan projects, budgets, and resources

❏ Act as liaison between key decision makers and clients

❏ Plan, coordinate, and organize

❏ Troubleshoot

❏ Envision

❏ Manage

2. What knowledge do I bring to a job and employer?

This is the body of information that you have accumulated through years of work that has led to your expertise or, if you are just out of school, the subjects and theories you know about.

Samples include:

❏ JavaScript, Enterprise, and SaaS platforms

❏ Hospital operations

❏ Gourmet cooking

❏ Cybersecurity

❏ Web analytics

❏ Animal husbandry

❏ Advanced manufacturing and materials

❏ Client-server and web technology

❏ Consultative sales

❏ Unmanned aerial systems

❏ Music theory, vocal coaching, and pedagogy

❏ Contingency planning and logistics

❏ Editing and proofreading

❏ Project management

❏ Social media

❏ Building codes

❏ Property management

❏ Retail store design

❏ Donor relations, fund-raising, and development

❏ Classroom management and curriculum planning

❏ Investor behavior and buying patterns

❏ IRS regulations

❏ Proposal writing

❏ Location scouting

❏ Printmaking and silk-screening

❏ Sales management

❏ Outsource management

❏ Landscape materials and installation

❏ Media relations and digital media marketing

❏ Small-business operations

❏ Horse breeding

❑ Financial planning and investment strategies

❑ Marketing, pricing, and distribution

❑ Consumer behavior

❑ Process improvement

❑ Customer service

❑ Conflict management

❑ Architectural design

❑ Geospatial information systems

❑ Commercial development

❑ Consumer packaging

❑ Statistics

❑ Risk assessment

3. What experience do I bring to an employer?
Describe by industry or general area of expertise.

Samples include:

❑ Advertising

❑ Government

❑ Transportation

❑ Aerospace

❑ Arts

❑ Biotech

❏ Telecommunications

❏ Healthcare

❏ Information technology

❏ Secondary education

❏ Administrative services and support

❏ Market research

❏ Finance

❏ Manufacturing operations

❏ Public relations

❏ Real estate

❏ Retail sales

❏ Technical support and service

❏ Human resources

❏ Engineering

❏ Law

❏ Consumer goods

❏ Nonprofit

Now let's go back to this question: *After you've left the room, how do you want to be seen and remembered?*

YOUR "HOW I WANT TO BE SEEN" PROFILE
Most likely you've checked off and come up with a lot of items in this exercise. Look at what you've written and pick out the words that

are most important and meaningful to you and that best describe
you. Then put them together in several brief statements to come up
with your "How I Want to Be Seen" Profile.

Here are a few examples to get you started.

I want to be seen as . . .

- a respected, passionate leader with a wealth of experience in
  information technology

. . . with the skills to:

- build trusting relationships

- train nontechnical types to understand technical processes

- troubleshoot

- anticipate client needs before they even know there's a problem

. . . with a reputation as:

- an innovative thinker and risk taker

- a caring mentor

- an early adopter

- a highly ethical professional

. . . who is not afraid of making mistakes.

I want to be seen as . . .

- a brilliant strategist with in-depth experience in marketing
  and social media

. . . with the skills to:

▫ organize disparate information into meaningful data

▫ research global competition

▫ write clear, concise reports

. . . who is known for:

▫ being an intuitive, empathetic listener

▫ being trustworthy

▫ always knowing how to handle difficult client situations

▫ having an insatiable curiosity for technology that generates usable information

▫ absolutely loving every aspect of taking a new product to market

I want to be seen as . . .

▫ a brilliant, budding economist who has dedicated my education to understanding how to create economic growth and raise the standard of living

. . . with the strengths to:

▫ analyze and solve complex economic programs related to profitability, economic modeling, and forecasting

▫ apply mathematical models

▫ effectively communicate economic theories and outcomes

▫ research business cycles and historical data

. . . who is known for:

▫ leading others

▫ working hard and playing hard

▫ never giving up

▫ being passionate about economic thought and methodology

Now you may be saying, "There sure is a lot of emphasis on those 'how you are' kinds of things. What about my hard-earned education that I'll be paying back with interest for the next 10 years? And it seems like my actual experience would matter more than anything."

Of course these matter. As I've said before—and as you summarized here—your functional skills, knowledge, and experience are part of the story. You can surely trot out all of that. And there will be plenty of chances to do so.

But let me remind you of something else we discussed in Chapter 1: You can have all the "right" experience, skills, and knowledge but not get past a phone screening or a first interview because of how else you *seem*. You may look great on paper, but seem in person like a belligerent toad or a complete misfit for a company's culture.

Here's a perfect example.

Alex Churchill knows exactly what he's looking for in every person he hires for his or his clients' companies. He helps companies like Rockstar Games, Adobe, and Microsoft find everything from Flash engineers—who work with Flash technology used on websites to add interactivity, animation, and video—to chief technology officers, environmental artists, and monetization experts.

When he looks at a candidate, education is a given. As he says, education is the door opener.

"We assume that a computer science degree from Stanford or Carnegie Mellon is going to provide an excellent level of education and knowledge," he says. But his clients—companies on the cutting edge of technology who pride themselves on innovation—are not just looking for someone with a computer science degree.

What will make you stand out from everyone else who has the same education? Your values and the characteristics that define how you operate, think, and will contribute. In this industry they're looking for people who are adventurous, risk takers, unafraid of failure, early adopters, and passionate about what the company does.

So if, for example, you're being considered for a particular engineering job at a social music start-up, you might have a computer science degree from Stanford and know oodles about back end and front end technology. But unless you are a fan of music, and can talk about it for 60 minutes, "You'll never get to work there no matter how good your programming skills are," Churchill says.

His own company has an entire division dedicated to recruiting people who work in social network gaming. They believe strongly in the "social network strategy." So as Churchill points out, "One of our values is that you've always got to be innovative."

If people don't demonstrate that they are innovative and moving forward in their thinking, they won't get far in the interview process. He was interviewing a man with a lot of industry experience and "one of the best resumes in the industry," says Churchill. But this man "couldn't see the benefit of being social, of bringing communities together. It was beyond him. He couldn't innovate. He couldn't adopt the strategy and move forward where things are going. When I talked to him about it, he looked at me like I was from Mars."

❝ *We become what we repeatedly do."*
—Sean Covey, author of *The 7 Habits of Highly Effective Teens*

On the other hand, a company will also know you have the right values when it sees them. At Yammer, the fast-growing San Francisco enterprise software firm also mentioned in Chapter 1, an important value is that employees voice their opinions and share ideas about company decisions, says Joe Cheung, director of recruiting.

How does he know it when he sees it in a potential worker? He says he can always tell "because during the interview they will ask a lot of questions and be more inquisitive about the organization and its culture. They ask about what it's like to work at Yammer, not about our salary and perks. Their biggest concern is about whether they can actually add value."

"See, It's Not Just Talk" Exercise

So far you've defined how you want to seem and you've put that together to create your "How I Want to Be Seen" Profile. With that tool in mind, let's think through what you would say and how you would act to make your Profile come to life at those three crucial connecting points.

Keep in mind that everything about you is fair game:

◻ Your personal appearance—your clothes, how you're groomed, and yes, even how you smell

◻ The actual words you speak and write, the composition of the letters, resumes, and other documents you create online, and even the very paper you print them on

◻ The way you treat others from the moment you enter an

office and handle yourself in every verbal exchange and interaction, and even when interruptions come up

So how are you going to show them you're not just talk?

1. WHEN FIRST CONTACTING AN EMPLOYER OR FOLLOWING UP ON AN INQUIRY

What would you say on the phone or write in your correspondence to illustrate how you want to be seen? What particular language would you use? Is there an achievement or experience you can summarize that illustrates how you've been one of the most creative thinkers in your past three jobs?

For example, let's say it is important for the employer to know how much you love technology and how it changes lives. Most people would say or write something like this:

"I really enjoy technology and being able to access information from anywhere."

That's nice. But several million other people enjoy those things too.

If you want to get attention, why not *illustrate* how you utilize and seek out technology in your own life? Why not really stand out and show what you mean by writing or saying something like this?

> I know for this role it is extremely important to have a fundamental love of technology and an understanding of how it can change your life. That certainly describes me. Besides being involved in world-class software development at work, I love incorporating technology in all areas of my life. As a runner, I use technology for my races and practices, which allows me to track my progress, train, and map out running courses. It not only makes running more fun, it makes me more effective.

Eric Zuckerman points out that you get nowhere portraying yourself like the rest of the world: "You and everyone else says, 'I work well in teams as well as individually' in their resume and in their letters."

But if you say, "I noticed your company works on such-and-that projects, which are similar to the such-and-such project I worked on . . . " or you point out how that project is something you studied and here's why it excites you, that in turn will get Zuckerman excited about you.

Doing this not only shows that you have the potential to do the job, but it "tells me you looked into our company and the position," Zuckerman says. It demonstrates some of those most desirable qualities: initiative and passion for the job and industry.

As another example, what details would you pay close attention to in your correspondence to convey that you are meticulous in your work and believe that presentation is everything?

Here's how one employer, Bill Strauss, noticed (and didn't notice) this quality as he was making his way through a batch of resumes and letters from people who had applied for a part-time marketing director job.

Strauss, chairman of the Cincinnati law firm Strauss & Troy, says he was looking for "a beckoning from behind the cold piece of paper."

Sorting through the top 12 prospects on a flight to Los Angeles, he says, "I was hoping to see a spark of creativity, some individuality that came through in the writing. But they were all so similar I had trouble keeping them distinctive in my head and they started to blur together."

So he started looking at the resume and application itself as a marketing piece, "as if this is an example of their work. I looked for typos, grammar, writing, and persuasion skills of the person who was in the act of marketing to me." He began nixing applicants right and left.

"I eliminated some at the most superficial level. They said they had editing and proofing in their skill set, but their bullet points weren't lined up. If someone started out the cover letter in an informal style by using a first name, it wasn't professional."

He found that one applicant's e-mail address itself was unprofessional and telling of the person. Grammatical errors turned him off. There were incorrect spellings such as "tecknical" and "Cincinnatti."

The applicant who stood out most and as best qualified to represent the firm "sent us an actual letter on stationery in a nice folder," says Strauss.

"It's superficial, I know. But it looked like a person who cared about the appearance of her work product"—an important value to this employer.

"When someone takes the time and trouble to send you a letter with a signature on letterhead, that stands out," he adds. "It's like a flower among weeds."

2. WHEN SITTING ACROSS FROM YOUR WOULD-BE BOSS OR HIRING MANAGER

What stories or examples would you share in your interviews to reinforce what you said in your correspondence or to make sure the employer knows about you?

For example, what achievements can you talk about that show how passionate you are about this work? What situation have you been in at work, in school, or in another place where you were eager to excel and made a difference?

What situations can you share that clearly show how you used your greatest strengths? What's an example of how you earned your reputation for always knowing how to deal with difficult situations and delicate subjects? And just as important: How will you live and breathe that in an interview?

Here's an example of how this job hunter did a poor job of demonstrating several important values. She wanted to be seen as a buttoned-down professional who pays attention to details, gives every project close scrutiny, and always plans for things that could go wrong.

She showed up at the interview with a button missing on the front of her blouse and a safety pin in its place. It may seem like a small thing, but that pin stood out like a sore thumb to the employer. When it came down to her and two other people, that teensy-weensy pin popping out of her blouse was the deciding factor. Another person who was equally qualified—but impeccably dressed—got the job.

As you already read in Chapter 1, Alex Churchill believes that hiring is not just about whether someone can do the job. "It's about taking on our culture. The people we hire are the ambassadors for VonChurch. We've got to have shared values," he says.

Here's how VonChurch begins to get at whether you share the company's values. When you arrive for an interview, you are offered a seat and a glass of water. "If you don't say thank you after being offered the water, you've failed the interview right there," says Churchill. Being polite is a core value at his company. And that's the first way the company decides whether you've got it.

3. WHEN FOLLOWING UP AFTER AN INTERVIEW
How will you reinforce what you just described?

What will you do to show how interested you are in this position? How will you continue to show the employer that you are passionate about this field?

For example, let's say you want to reinforce your research skills, initiative, and willingness to go beyond the call of duty. During the interview, you learned about a new product the company is thinking about launching or a new service that is still in the research phase.

Why not do some digging into this? Is any other company doing something like it? Who's the company's competition? What's happening in the marketplace that makes this a viable product or service? Find out the answers to these questions and then, along with your well-written thank-you letter, summarize the relevant information you discovered. Maybe even add in a few ideas of your own. You'll be showing and reinforcing your functional skills, enthusiasm, interest in the work, and initiative.

AND ONE MORE THING . . .

What do you want to be careful *not* to say or do at any of these three points in the process so that you can avoid giving the opposite impression of how you want to seem?

There are just some things you want to make sure you don't discuss or do. You know, something like this:

"The reason I left my last job is because my boss and I never saw eye to eye. In fact, the guy was such a moron he fired me when I came up with a plan that would cut expenses in our department by 60 percent. He was so threatened, he couldn't stand that I was smarter than him."

You might be a bit worried about that slipping out.

But here's the thing. The fact that you're worried about *not* saying something like that can prevent you from keeping that unwanted thought or behavior at bay, says Sian Beilock, a psychologist and author of the book *Choke* (Free Press, 2010).

Here's what happens in your head: You're trying hard *not* to think about something, right? But two things are going on in your brain, she says, drawing on the work of Harvard psychologist Daniel Wegner.

There's the conscious search for the unwanted thought. But

under pressure, only the unconscious works. So you're more likely to blurt out what you're trying not to say or do. How annoying is that?

In order to help you not say or do what you don't want to say or do, Beilock suggests writing out your worries so they don't intrude when the pressure is on. That's why I want you to write down *what you want to be careful not to say or do*. So you won't choke when the pressure is on.

There's No Stopping You Now

Congratulations. You did the hard work.

- You thought through how you want to seem.

- You've begun to explore what you'll *tell* the employer so the company sees you that way, and then what you'll do to *show* you are actually that way—so it's not just talk.

Now that you've gone through these exercises, you'll be hard to miss.

For starters, millions of other job hunters haven't done this. *So you'll stand out.* You'll also be focused on demonstrating the qualities employers look for (how could they resist such a passionate, considerate professional who gets along well with others, knows her stuff, and can handle difficult clients?) and the ones you want them to be sure to see. They can't help but take notice—in a good way.

You'll be setting yourself apart from everyone else you're competing with at those three crucial connecting points—before, during, and after an interview.

In your initial contact, you'll be demonstrating the very skills you say you have in your correspondence and written materials. As a result, employers will say, "Hmm, she seems like she's on the ball.

She thinks like us. She's the got the right attitude. Let's contact her and set up a phone or face-to-face interview."

During the interview, you'll be ready to ask questions that demonstrate such things as your intellectual curiosity and desire to be part of something bigger than yourself. You'll be ready to respond to the interviewer's questions in ways that show you have the right skills and sensitivity to client needs to get the job done. The way you treat everyone will show how well you fit.

As a result, employers will say, "I liked her. She was sharp, articulate, considerate, and very positive. I can tell she's got the skills the job calls for and seems to be the kind of person we need. Let's bring her back for a second interview."

You've begun to think through how you'll reinforce the impression you made in the interview and in your follow-up. So now an employer will say, "Yes, she is just as I had hoped. She not only has the technical skills we need, she's got the right attitude and values. She does what she says she's going to do. She fits in. I feel I can trust and rely on her."

You are prepared to convey this: *What I told you and what you see is what you get.*

It's not that hard to stand out when you're acting differently from everyone else. And that's a good thing.

Was It Good for You?

A couple of years ago I heard an interview with Warren Buffett, CEO of Berkshire Hathaway, one of the wealthiest people and most successful investors on the planet. When asked how he decides whether to buy a business, he said, "We get a letter from someone, then we meet in person, which verifies and multiplies what I thought when I got the first letter." Then he looks at this: "Did the meeting reinforce what I thought initially?"

> *In other words, he asks himself,* Is this someone I want to be in business with? *His decision is based on the* experience *he has with that person.*
>
> *This is no different from the process used by an employer who's trying to decipher whether you are a good fit. That person too is asking the same question:* Is this someone I want to be in business with or be a part of my business? *Like Buffett, the* decision is based on the experience the employer has with you.
>
> *So all of it comes down to this question:*
>
> What experience do you want the employer to have with you so that the company will want to do business with you?

YOUR "HOW I WANT TO BE SEEN" REGULATOR

When I asked my clients to think through the three questions in the "See, It's Not Just Talk" Exercise, it always feels a little foreign at first. Most of us just don't sit around and think of ourselves in such precise language. We simply enter conversations, respond to others, and get on with our work without thinking about how we are "being."

By thinking through what you believe, what you stand for, and what you do, you now know yourself better, can feel it through and through, and are ready to live and breathe it at every juncture of the job-hunting process.

Your "How I Want to Be Seen" Regulator—which helps you know what to say and do at any given moment—is now more finely tuned. This is especially key under stressful conditions.

Mark my words, you're more equipped to consciously choose how to be and can turn your values into habits, which determine how things go.

As Mahatma Gandhi said so well:

Your beliefs become your thoughts,

Your thoughts become your words,

Your words become your actions,

Your actions become your habits,

Your habits become your values,

Your values become your destiny.

Now, with your "How I Want to Be Seen" Profile under your belt, let's look at specific situations you'll find yourself in during a job hunt. In the next chapter we'll focus on what you'll *do* and *not do* so you will indeed leave the room the way you want to be seen and remembered.

three

□ □ □ □ □ □ □ □ □ □

15 Things You Should Never Do

You've got three big chances to open—and keep open—the door called Juicy New Opportunity with an employer. Remember when those times are? That's right. Before, during, and after the interview.

Here are 15 things you don't ever want to do at these times. Do them and you will almost guarantee that the door will never open or will be abruptly slammed shut in your face (usually with no explanation) shortly thereafter. And, of course, along with what *not* to do, here is what to *do* instead.

Some of these don'ts and do's require more explanation than others. Some occur before, during, or after an interview. Others will overlap, while some may bleed into things to say and not say. If they do, fear not, I go into detail about the things you should never talk about or say in the next chapter.

Wherever you are in the job hunting process, please keep this critical, prevailing principle in the back of your mind:

"Getting a job" is not the objective of a job interview.

You read that right. "Getting a job" is not what you're there for. Or it shouldn't be if you want to be successful in this process.

Here's why. The fact is, one or more crazy busy people have pulled out their calendars and juggled five other meetings and three projects to get you on their schedule. This meeting of the minds is not an invitation to give you a job. *It's an opportunity to hold a conversation.*

It's the chance to meet and get to know you. To see how you think and how you seem. And to know if it makes sense to explore more. You've piqued their interest. The door has been opened and they're peering through a tiny crack. That's all.

Plus, *you* don't even know if you want the job yet. Really. Think about it. You don't. How could you so soon? You don't have enough information. You need to have this conversation to do the same thing: to get to know the employer. To see how they think and seem. And explore whether it's right for *you*.

Yes, even if you've been out of work for some time and are giddy to get an offer after months of no paycheck, or one that will sweep you away from a bad situation. Without a real conversation, the words "When can I start?" will be out of your mouth before you know it. And within months, you may be back to pounding the pavement—these days, more like the computer keys—to take you away from your new workplace from hell.

So treat it like the special, get-to-know-each-other opportunity it is. This may seem like a small distinction. But it's quite important. For if you understand that, when you contact or respond to an employer, you'll go into interviews and follow up feeling more relaxed and less stressed. And I promise, that will let you focus on this sole objective: *To explore whether the company and the job are right for you and you are right for the company while presenting yourself in the best possible light.*

This is *so* important and fundamental to everything we'll cover from this point on. Come to think of it, we should do something this very second so you won't forget it. Yes, let's do that: Retype or write the following on a piece of paper and post it where you'll see it:

My objective is to explore whether the company and the job are right for me and I am right for the company while presenting myself in the best possible light.

Got it?

Also, keep your "How I Want to Be Seen" Profile handy as you read through this chapter.

So to be able to achieve your objective and move the process to the next step, *don't* do the following 15 things.

#1: Don't Act Clueless and Unprepared

I guarantee you will act clueless, be unprepared, and not be in that "exploring" frame of mind to present yourself in the best possible light if you don't have some very specific data about three things:

1. The company

2. The job

3. Yourself

Let's say you're out and about in the world and you meet an employer who says, "Contact me." Or you want to initiate contact with someone you've never met at a particular company.

If you're clueless about what the company does, how on earth can you 1) get anyone interested in scheduling that meeting, 2) have an intelligent conversation about the company and how you can contribute, and 3) fit the interviewer's preconception of whether you can do the job—any job—if you know nothing about the company? How can you determine whether the company and job are right for you and you are right for the company while presenting yourself in the best possible light? You can't.

WHAT TO KNOW ABOUT THE COMPANY

□ Does it manufacture a product or offer a service? What exactly is that product or service? What does it do? Who buys it and why? What problems does the product or service solve?

□ What are the company's overall goals?

□ What's the company's sales volume, if applicable?

□ What's the culture like?

□ Who's the competition?

□ Who runs the company and what is its overall management philosophy?

When I ask my clients these questions about a company they want to approach or are preparing to interview with, 85 percent of the time they reply, "Well, I'm not exactly sure what they do. I think they do such-and-such, but I'm not clear."

I want to scream. But I don't. I just sigh very loudly.

Maybe you're so excited to actually hear back from an employer and you're not thinking straight. Or heaven forbid, you're being lazy. Whatever the reason, if you do initiate contact in a state of cluelessness, you will end up wasting the opportunity and sending a vague, off-base initial e-mail like this one: "I am following up as you suggested after we met at the workshop. I would love an opportunity to start my career with a company like yours."

What's wrong with that, you ask? For starters, companies aren't in business to give you an opportunity to start your career. *They are in business to manufacture a product or offer a service. They hire people who can help them achieve that.*

Plus, here's your big chance to grab the company by the throat—figuratively speaking of course—and show that you're 100 times more savvy, passionate, and qualified than everyone else.

When you lack this information about the company, you might as well be saying (and some people actually do say), "I heard your company is looking for someone. I am available."

So what if you're available? So are millions of other people.

Harsh, but true.

George Bradt—who today is managing director of the executive onboarding consulting firm PrimeGenesis—asked a simple question of the mid-level manager he was interviewing when he was CEO of Power Information Network: "What do you know about me?"

"He didn't know anything," says Bradt.

The very question, he says, "gets at motivation. What I'm really asking is, 'Prove to me that you care enough about this job to have done some basic research.' What concerned me about this individual's not knowing anything about me was that it meant he had not even looked at our company's website, let alone done any more research. This screamed a lack of motivation."

Show up to an interview without knowing about the company's goals, culture, products, or services and there you'll be, sitting eyeball-to-eyeball with an employer, doomed to make totally awful comments such as these:

"I don't really know what you do but . . . "

"What exactly do you do here?"

"I know you work with sick people, but that's about it."

"I heard you were a good company to work for."

I did not make these up.

CEO Rob Basso says that when it comes to knowing about his company, "Most people are not prepared at the level we would like to see. They do not do the research on our company, its history, or who they are interviewing with."

How does this grab him? It's not good news for the laggards.

"This demonstrates a huge lack of initiative," he says.

Remember back to Chapter 1 and the list of qualities and characteristics employers want? "Self-initiative" was #7 on the list.

But "those who take the time to find out about our company and can have a discussion about our marketing campaigns, branding efforts, and recent press, they are a step ahead of their competition," says Basso.

Did you catch that? "Ahead of their competition." That's where you want to be. And it's quite doable.

WHAT TO KNOW ABOUT THE JOB

- What the job is (if a specific one exists)

- Who it reports to

- What issues and problems it addresses

Early on—before the interview—you may not know what particular job a company has open or thinks you could fit. But did you ask?

Most of the time when I ask my clients *this* question, they tell me that they have not done so. I don't know why this doesn't occur to them. They seem to think employers will be annoyed and get mad if they ask. I ask them, "What could be so upsetting about this question?" They don't know. That's because there's nothing to get upset about.

I assure you, it is a perfectly reasonable request. And it's one you must ask to meet that objective you just posted on your wall.

When you know nothing about the job and its responsibilities, you lose the opportunity to illustrate how you are a match. Plus, you'll end up saying things that make you seem clueless, which will then hurt your chances of getting an offer. Here are a few examples of cluelessness I've heard lately:

"I don't believe in spending half my time doing social media." (What if the job entails doing social media half the day?)

"I just want a job where I can work eight hours and have my evenings and weekends free." (This is just a dumb thing to say no matter what. You can always negotiate these issues later. And what if the job requires you to work one evening a month? When you come across as this inflexible and focused on *your* needs, you're not helping your cause.) Think back to the list of what employers want (Chapter 1). Flexibility and adaptability is #13 on that list.

"I don't know much about environmental stuff." (What if knowing and caring about the environment is key to this job or is one of the company's core values?)

The worst thing is going to an interview and not even knowing what job you're discussing.

In the first minutes of an interview PacTeam Group President Eric Zuckerman had with one woman, she said: "I'm sorry, what was this position? I've been on so many interviews. Can you remind me which position I'm interviewing for?"

"That's when the conversation ended," he says.

Even after you've asked the person who interviewed you by phone, the recruiter, or whoever scheduled the interview, you may feel you know little about the job. So at least know what you're good at and love to do and where you see yourself fitting into an organization.

WHAT TO KNOW ABOUT YOURSELF

- Your "How I Want to Be Seen" Profile from Chapter 2, which includes:
  - your top strengths and talents
  - the knowledge that makes you an expert or familiar with the type of issues the job deals with
  - a summary of your experience
  - key qualities, characteristics, attitudes, and philosophies that help you fit this role
- Examples of how you've applied all of this successfully in the past in a paid or unpaid position.

Wouldn't you like to say intriguing things that will entice an employer to want to meet? Knowing information about the company, *plus* yourself, will do that. Here's an example of how you can do this in your initial contact with an employer (you could write this in a note or say it on the phone):

> I was fascinated by your work in third world countries. When I was a Peace Corps volunteer, I saw firsthand how a product like yours can make a difference. I would love to meet to find out more about your goals and explore how my background in medical devices can help you meet them.

Isn't that a lot better than "I heard you are hiring"? But you'd never know to say the former if you didn't do your homework.

If you don't know about the position and can't talk effectively about yourself, you can't very well explain why you'd like the job or whether you'd be a good fit for it. And this will lead you to say other inane things, like "I'd like a job where I'm in a nice office and work for a good company." (One of my clients actually said this when I asked him what position he wanted.) Or, "I have a lot of experience and am a good communicator and team player." (Do you know how many other people say those exact words? You can do much better than that.)

Most people cannot describe the job they want, says Dianne Durkin of Loyalty Factor. "They'll say they can do anything. So I ask them, 'What are you really good at?' When I tell them to go away and figure out what their primary strengths are, I usually never hear back."

Others can't even describe their fundamental skills. These are the basics that qualify you to do a job. For instance, the fundamentals for a financial planner are the ability to translate financial data so the average person knows what you're talking about.

The basics also include knowledge. For example, certain types of engineering jobs require you know about equipment specifications and electronic circuitry.

Know *your* fundamentals.

Young Workers, New Grads, and Career Changers— Be Especially Wary

This acting clueless business can be a big issue with younger workers, new graduates, or someone moving into an area in which they've never worked.

For example, most employers say that after interviewing dozens of new grads, they find these young people are bright, they like technology, and they know about social media. But when asked to explain what they'd like to do at the company, they say the same thing: "I want to learn."

Saying that might make you sound eager, which isn't a bad thing. But if that's all you've got to offer, well, let's just say it's doubtful you'll make the cut.

Of course if you are coming right out of college or making a career change, you only know so much about the field you're trying to get into. You'll get no argument from these employers that there will be plenty to learn. They are willing to teach you the ropes. But that's not why they'd hire you.

Why would they hire you? Because you can help them create and deliver the product they make or service they offer. However, they are not in the business of teaching. It is a cold fact of the work world that every organization—for-profit, nonprofit, government, or healthcare—is in the business of delivering a service or product.

To get hired, you'd better know how you'll help them do that. Put another way: How will you justify your paycheck?

Even if you don't know exactly what you want to do for a company or exactly what a job entails, there is no excuse for going to interviews unprepared. None. It's a matter of understanding their business and your talents. I go into detail on this in Chapter 4.

SO WOULD A LITTLE RESEARCH KILL YOU?

Spend *at least* a half an hour (preferably more) reviewing the company's website *before you make contact*. The more you know, the more prepared you'll be. And that, I guarantee, will naturally lead you to feel more excited about the company and the job.

Having said that, I'm the first to point out that a lot of company websites are, well, let's put it this way—not easy to navigate. They focus on selling their products and they love, love, love industry lingo. Half the time, you can't figure out what they do. So you'll have to really dig around to figure out what it all means.

In general, look for a tab or section that says "Our Company"—which many times isn't at the top of the page, but the bottom. Then it's a matter of more digging.

Let's say you've got an interview at Pitney Bowes. On its website, the company describes itself as "a $5.6 billion company that employs 33,000 worldwide and provides software, hardware and services that integrate physical and digital communications channels."

Do you know what this means? I sure don't.

If you snoop around you'll find out what their business makes. Things like the Olympus II Incoming Mail Sorting Solution, which helps with "labor-intensive sorting of incoming mail" that can be "costly and error-prone." This Olympus II helps a company "save time and money by automating your inbound letter and flats sorting at speeds up to 36,000 pieces per hour." Now I'm getting the picture.

I bet you didn't know Pitney Bowes was inducted into the Environmental Protection Agency's WasteWise Hall of Fame—"one of the many ways we've been recognized for our leadership, diversity, innovation and environmental stewardship." Check out the Awards & Recognition section and you'll get a sense of what the company cares about. Depending on the kind of work you do, this could be good to know.

Pitney Bowes also talks about its four-pronged approach to product development and innovative milestones, starting with the first postage meter back in 1902 and continuing up to the hybrid digital signature scheme. This can be good material for small talk and more.

For more insight into a company's leaders, look for "Leadership & Governance," then drill down to "Corporate Officers." And don't forget there's always LinkedIn profiles to learn more information about a particular person.

On Pitney Bowes's site there's also a letter and video from CEO Murray Martin. Yes, it's filled with the typical gobbledygook like "create value," "emerging opportunities," "commitment to integrity and service," and "innovative technologies." But it gives you a feel for the place and the players, making it easier to not show up clueless.

Even if it has the worst website on the planet, there's no excuse for not knowing something about a company. Just do a web search on it. Something, somewhere will have been written about the company, its products or services, the owners, or the management.

To learn more about the job, ask: "Could you tell me more details about the job? What are the responsibilities? Who does it report to?" Don't be shy.

Don't

▫ Contact employers or go into interviews clueless about what a company does, who runs it and what it's known for, the job, and how you can help the business.

Employers will conclude . . .

▫ You only care about yourself.

▫ You're lazy, careless, and lack initiative.

▫ You don't understand or care about their business, the job, or the industry.

▫ You lack intellectual curiosity and critical thinking skills.

▫ You don't know yourself and how you can contribute.

- Your judgment is questionable.

- You don't value their time.

- You don't care about growing with the company.

- They'll end up spending too much time teaching you since you don't seem to have a grasp of the business.

- You're just looking for a place where you can soak up everything they have to teach you, get trained, and then leave.

Do

- Know what the company does, its history, leaders, philosophy, and culture.

- Know what the job is and where you'd fit, and review this thoroughly before your interview.

- Help the employer precisely connect the dots between what it needs and what you can do for the company.

- Understand and point out how your contribution will pay for itself once you've mastered the basics.

#2: Don't Get Defensive

What's there to get defensive about? Plenty. Here are a few questions that could rub you the wrong way.

"Why aren't you working now?" "Why'd you leave your last job?" "Why didn't you work for five years?" "Why'd you have eight jobs in five years?"

Feeling a little combative?

There's a good reason for everything that has happened to you in your career. Some of it undoubtedly is touchy. Some things you'd just rather not talk about, right? Other issues take some explaining. As a result—and depending on what happened and how you feel about it—your response can end up sounding aggressive or angry. Even raise suspicion that you're covering something up. The very word "Why" makes some job hunters jumpy.

Dianne Durkin noticed people got so defensive about such questions as "Why did you stay at this job for this long?" or "Why did you leave when you did?" that her company eliminated "why" questions from the interview process.

But most employers will ask why this and why that. It's reasonable. If you were them, wouldn't you want to understand where you've been and why?

If you've been unemployed a while, they may wonder if your skills and know-how have languished. Whether you'll stay if they pour thousands of dollars into training you or leave when something better comes along. And they may ask about your period of unemployment in order to get other insights into what kind of worker you'd be.

"I often notice the time someone has been unemployed," says Eric Zuckerman. "Has it been five months or two years? If it is the latter, I may question why they have not been working for so long and what they have been doing meanwhile. Have they been doing volunteer work or just sitting at the computer 'looking for a job'? I like to see somebody who has been proactive during their unemployment because that tells me that they would be proactive when working for me."

Overall, the fact that someone is or is not employed is not the issue—it's the reason a person is unemployed that is most telling, he says.

"If a person worked in an industry that got hit hard during the recession and they have been laid off because the company did drastic downsizing, I am not going to hold that against them," he says. "At the same time, I will expect the person to come to me with positive energy, excited for the future and determined to succeed."

Translation: If you get defensive explaining where you've been, for how long, and why—especially if something negative occurred— you won't be showing that positive energy, excitement for the future, and determined-to-succeed attitude he's looking for (#6 on that list from Chapter 1).

Other times it's *how* an employer asks a question that can get you riled.

"Why have you been out of a job so long?" Whoa. Who said you have been out of a job so long?

Or how about this one: "Why is it taking you so long to find a new position?" Or "What kind of trouble did you have with your last boss?" All of these are negatively stated questions that may make you want to put up your dukes.

Even when the question is not asked in a negative way, nearly every employer I talked to noted how often people get defensive when they dig into their resume and past experiences. And guess what that did?

"It definitely skews your perception of whether or not they are being honest and if I should continue to consider them for the position," says Rob Basso.

It's one thing to say, "I don't want to get into what happened at my last job"— which would likely raise suspicion. It's another to say, "I enjoyed my job at the Red Bird Company for 10 years. When they were bought out by a large corporation, I decided to leave and work for a smaller firm where I could have more day-to-day impact."

It makes perfect sense to ask about your past. How else will they get to know you?

They're not looking for squeaky clean. They are looking for a reasonable explanation about where you've been and why, and what brings you to where you are today. And how you discuss it will reveal a lot about you.

So expect to be asked.

Don't

▫ Hedge, fudge, get mad, out-and-out refuse to respond, or lie.

Employers will conclude . . .

▫ You're not being honest.

▫ You're angry and defensive.

▫ You've got something to hide.

▫ You have a bad attitude.

▫ You'll be difficult to deal with on the job.

▫ You may not handle criticism well.

Do

▫ Look at every job you've had. Think through and prepare what you'll say that explains what happened in a factual, objective way that doesn't raise more questions.

▫ Understand why they're asking questions and respond with objective information.

#3: Don't Ever, Ever Be Late

This may seem obvious. But apparently it's not. Which baffles me.

I say this from my experience with so many late people. You set a time and date to meet. Be there. On time. What's so hard about that? Employers would like to know this too.

Nearly 40 percent of the time people are late to interviews with Eric Zuckerman.

If you are late for a meeting with Dianne Durkin and you don't call to say you're lost, you "lose credibility with me," she says. "It tells me you may not be dedicated at work either."

"I've had candidates who do not show up at all with no call or e-mail warning," says Rob Basso. If you're running late and call to let him know that, Basso will give you the benefit of the doubt. But, he says, "Show up late to an interview without advance warning and I have to assume this is a reoccurring trait." And that you think being late is acceptable.

How much do employers hate late people?

In its 2009 poll, the Society for Human Resource Management asked nearly 500 employers this question: "How detrimental would being late for the interview be to getting the job?" Fifty-eight percent said it's a deal breaker and 39 percent said it's somewhat of a problem. That's 97 percent.

"All of that over such a small thing?" you say. A businessperson's time is no minor thing. Someone carved out a time slot for you. Respect that.

And while we're on the subject of time, don't waste it once you get to an interview either. Come prepared with an extra copy or two of your resume in hand. Yes, it's possible that the employer misplaced yours in that stack of 562 other resumes it got. Here's a chance to show how considerate and efficient you are.

Don't

- Wait until the last minute to find out where you're going.

- Make excuses for being late.

Employers will conclude . . .

▫ You don't know how to plan and think ahead.

▫ You're disrespectful of their time.

▫ You won't take your work seriously or don't care that much about your work.

▫ You're not dedicated.

Do

▫ Give yourself an extra half hour to get to an interview, taking into consideration traffic, construction, and parking.

▫ Get directions and scope out the location of the company— even do a test drive the day before.

▫ Arrive about ten minutes early. Go to the restroom and check to make sure everything is in place. And ladies, make sure there's no lipstick on your teeth.

#4: Don't Worry

I say this with great empathy. I worry about most things. I learned it from my mother, who learned it from her mother, who probably learned it from her mother before they ever set foot in this country. But it won't help you in an interview.

Yes, the stakes are high and the pressure is on big-time. And yes, most likely, you're worried about messing up and saying the wrong thing.

Performing poorly or worse than expected happens to a lot of highly competent people. But listen to this: Ironically, your desire to succeed can cause you to do your worst. So says Sian Beilock, psychologist and author of *Choke* (Free Press, 2010). All because you're worried.

Choking can occur when you think *too* much about an activity that is usually automatic. You've heard of paralysis by analysis?

Beilock does experiments with people in high-pressure situations at her Human Performance Lab at the University of Chicago. She says that under pressure, worry floods the brain. Try to suppress it and you *divert* brainpower. Which means you can't use your "working memory" or cognitive horsepower. And that's what lets you hold information in your mind while doing something else at the same time—like having a persuasive give-and-take *conversation* with a potential employer.

So what did I tell you? *Don't worry*. Find that sweet spot between being well prepared and not overthinking everything.

By the way, it also doesn't help to worry about the general state of affairs and go around saying, "There aren't any jobs" or "This process is so overwhelming, I'll never get anywhere." Trash talk about the economy and your prospects of finding a job would turn anyone into a crab. Which is not the kind of person employers like to hire.

To maintain a cheerier disposition, I highly recommend you *not* pay attention to the figures released on the first Friday of every month by the U.S. Labor Department, which point out things like the unemployment rate.

First, what difference do these numbers make to you and your job search? This short-term snapshot of estimated numbers, which are revised—sometimes dramatically—from previous months, only seems to irritate folks, which leads to this conclusion: "It's impossible to find a job."

As we talked about in Chapter 1, finding a job is not impossible. And as of this writing, the monthly report actually shows the job market getting better. But when it comes to your job search, these numbers are irrelevant. And with all the commentary that goes on every time they come out, it can put you into a counterproductive tizzy and negative frame of mind.

So it pays to examine how your perception can affect your performance in your job search.

You've heard of the power of positive thinking, right? Now psychologists believe there's such a thing as the *power of positive perception*.

Studies at Purdue University that looked at how perception affects performance found there's a clear relationship between how hard a task seems to be and how it actually appears.

One of the Purdue studies looked at golf and the hole on the green and how people *perceived* the hole. When people perceived the hole to be bigger, they made their putts more successfully, says Jessica Witt, associate professor of psychology at Colorado State University, who led the study when she was at Purdue University. The study results, titled "Get Me Out of This Slump! Visual Illusions Improve Sports Performance," were published in the April 2012 issue of *Psychological Science*.

"These effects aren't specific to athletes," Witt said on NPR's *Morning Edition* (April 18, 2012). "We find them in everybody, in all kinds of tasks. So if you have to walk up a hill to get to work, if you're tired or low energy and wearing a heavy backpack, that hill looks steeper or a distance looks farther."

And, as Witt pointed out, with positive perception comes confidence. In other words, "If the hill doesn't seem too steep or the golf hole appears bigger than it really is, that altered perception gives you confidence in your abilities," summed up Joe Palca of NPR in the interview.

So yes, think through what you'll say and anticipate issues. But also work on strengthening the power you have to see things in a more positive light.

Don't

- Overthink and plan every single thing you'll say and excessively worry about saying the wrong thing.

- Dwell on the general negative state of affairs.

Employers will conclude . . .

- You're not someone they feel comfortable being around.

- You're a negative influence.

Do

- Think through the questions you'll hear; plan and rehearse your general responses; and then go with the flow.

#5: Don't Act Old

I may be chronologically "old" to a 20- or 30-year old. But I don't see it. And I'll be darned if anyone else thinks that about me. And that's what matters most in this job-hunting business—how you see yourself.

No question, there is discrimination against older workers. No employer will say they won't hire you because of your age. But sometimes, you just know that's the reason.

However, there's also no question you won't get anywhere if you have decided "I'll never get hired at my age" or if you fear that employers think you're washed up.

There's only so much you can do, but—and this is a big but—you can help employers see you as more youthful and energetic, and therefore just as valuable, by how you think, what you say, and how you look.

You may have gotten a brush-off because an employer didn't

believe you're up to the task. But despite bad vibes or out-and-out rejection from some, there are plenty of companies that cherish your depth of wisdom, loyalty, and work ethic.

When conversing with people in general and potential employers in particular, pay close attention to how you talk about yourself. Do you sound like you're stuck in the past? Do you put a lot of emphasis on what you've done *before*? Your skills and knowledge are valuable, but you need to help employers see how what you know can help them *today*.

The challenge is to have the right balance of confidence and openness to learning new things. So you don't want to:

- Show "technical hesitation," as a consultant I interviewed for my column called it. This is when you convey a lack of familiarity or comfort with new technology.

- Have a sense of superiority. This is when you come across to a younger interviewer as condescending, or overly confident that you know exactly how to do something.

Even if you've done a particular task a hundred times, a new company may want it done differently. So you want to demonstrate your competence but also your willingness to approach things in different ways.

You don't want to do what one employer in Alabama told me some older candidates do: "They want to tell me what I should do with my company."

What do older workers have that gets them hired over younger workers? Strong interpersonal skills. This includes the good habit of making eye contact, really listening, and then solving someone's particular problem.

Because some employers have the perception that it's difficult for younger managers to oversee older workers, it's important that you show you take a collaborative approach. Some of the most successful younger boss/older worker relationships are based on mutual respect and appreciation for the other person. One 43-year-old who reports to a 31-year-old told me their relationship works in part because they realize that "We both have things to learn from one another."

Another plus for older workers is a realistic and mature outlook and sense of humor. One employer told me that she asked an older worker to describe a recent mistake he made. He just grinned, saying, "Do you want one from this week or last week?" Then he gave a good example, which included what he had learned from the error.

It may seem minor, but how do you look? Are you wearing the same glasses you've had for 15 years? Do your hairstyle and clothing look outdated? Are your clothes worn-looking or several sizes too small? It all plays into how an employer sees you.

More than anything, much of the time, how you'll be treated will depend on how you see yourself and present yourself. If you're not buying into the "They think I'm too old" issue, there's less chance an employer will. Your age is irrelevant. If you've done your part to not let it be an issue, a smart employer won't be deterred either.

Don't

- Fall into the trap of believing no one wants you because they'll think you're too old.

- Say things that make you seem outdated, like "I'm not very good with that kind of technology."

- Dwell on your extensive experience from the past.

- Display a sense of superiority.

- Act like you know it all or have a "my way or the highway" attitude.

- Think your experience should speak for itself.

- Tell employers what to do with their company.

- Look frumpy and dumpy.

Employers will conclude . . .

- You're inflexible.

- Your skills aren't up-to-date.

- You will be difficult to manage—especially by a younger person.

- You're stuck in the past.

Do

- Learn what you need to be up-to-date in your skills.

- Be and show you're open to new approaches.

- Respect others' expertise—especially if they're younger.

- Spruce up your clothes, hair, and physique to look healthy and vigorous. Get new glasses.

- Link your experience to the employer's current needs.

- Be open to what you can learn from younger workers.

- Look for opportunities to display a mature, realistic attitude and sense of humor.

#6: Don't Be Humble

I know your mother taught you not to brag. So did mine. But to sit back and hope your experience and resume speak for themselves won't cut it. And you're not helping matters by shriveling up in your interview chair when an employer challenges you or asks you tough questions.

If you aren't totally in love with yourself and your abilities and prepared to act like it, how can you inspire someone else to believe in you?

Even a 2012 study published in the *Journal of Applied Social Psychology* found that a little narcissism can't hurt. The word sounds pretty despicable, I know. It's a trait most people would never want. But the study found that a little self-admiration pays off in the short-term context of a job interview.

The University of British Columbia and University of Nebraska–Lincoln, which conducted this survey, discovered that narcissists scored much higher in simulated job interviews than did non-narcissists. Pointing to narcissists' innate tendency to promote themselves in part by engaging and speaking at length, the study found that their behavior implied confidence and expertise.

An interview is "one setting where it's OK to say nice things about yourself and there are no ramifications," says Peter Harms, assistant professor of management at the University of Nebraska–Lincoln and a co-author of the study.

"In fact, it's expected," he says. And those who are comfortable doing this tend to do much better than those who aren't.

The study showed that these types were not only more likely to self-promote, but when challenged by an interviewer, they "tend to double down" to make themselves look better, Harms says. "It's as if they say, 'Oh, you're going to challenge me? Then I'm not just great, I'm fantastic,' And in this setting, it tended to work."

The bottom line is that chronic self-promoters—those who spoke quickly and at length and used "ingratiation tactics such as smiling, gesturing and complimenting others"—were more highly rated. Equally qualified applicants who were more modest scored lower.

Just to be clear, I'm not suggesting you turn into an egomaniac before, during, or after the interview. But don't be afraid to talk proudly about your accomplishments. When describing a project, instead of saying "we" did this or that, take credit for your portion.

What's wrong with saying, "I put together a team that grew the territory from 20 to 50 accounts and $500 million in sales"? Or "I spearheaded the new department of 16 salespeople who handled $1.5 million in sales the first year"?

If you believe in yourself, don't shy away from saying so.

Don't

▫ Talk about what "we" did.

▫ Shrink back when you hear a challenging question.

Employers will conclude . . .

▫ You lack confidence.

▫ You lack initiative.

Do

▫ Get darn good at talking about yourself.

▫ Talk proudly and specifically about your skills, experience, beliefs, and ideas about how you helped other organizations and can help this one too.

▫ Use the "I" word.

#7: Don't Act Blasé, Unresponsive, and Disinterested

Michael Zwick, president of Assets International, always starts the interview by explaining what the company does and a bit about the role. Then he asks, "Any questions?"

If all you ask about is hours, pay, and benefits, you will have made it clear to him you aren't really interested in the job and his company. (I'll get into the pay and benefits issue in Chapter 4.)

Not asking thoughtful questions about his business is also a clue for Darrell Benatar, CEO of UserTesting.com, which receives hundreds of applications for customer service, administrative, and other specialized positions per week.

"People are effectively making an investment when they go to work for a company, so we want to hear the kind of questions an investor might have," he says.

Eric Zuckerman appreciates a curious mind and people who ask such questions as, "What kind of projects are you working on? Who would I get to work with?" But he sees few people who do that. "They may be interested, but they are aren't communicating it by the way they act," he says.

So shower employers with thoughtful, appropriate questions. Good ways to probe include asking:

- What are the key responsibilities of the job?

- What types of problems does this role address?

- What are the expectations of the position?

- What does it take to be successful?

- Why is this position open?

- What is a typical day or week like?

◻ How does this position contribute to the company, goals, innovation, productivity, or profits?

◻ How does your company see itself competing in the international market (if applicable)?

Specific questions about the job or company aren't the only way to show your interest. Mention a news item or trends that affect the industry or company. That will lead to more conversation. It can turn into an interesting back-and-forth, plus give you a chance to exhibit your intellectual curiosity and excitement about the work the company does (#10 and #5 on that list of what employers want in Chapter 1).

When you do get a nibble from an employer, don't wait to respond. Before you know it, a week has gone by. And by then, you've lost the momentum and the employer may have moved on.

Remember how Zuckerman said he assumes lack of response means lack of interest? Even if he hears excuses—"My computer was down"; "I had a funeral (an operation, a family emergency, a sick child)"; "I was out of the country"—it makes no difference. He has moved on.

Lack of responsiveness and other lackadaisical behavior also makes the employer wonder, "Will this person be that way on the job?"

The chance to respond occurs at various times throughout the job-hunting process. A small-business owner who was hiring her first employee had an interview with a man who really impressed her. To help her get a sense of his work, the candidate volunteered to work on a project over the weekend.

The employer and her partner met with the candidate again, at which time they asked him to think about working on the project full-time through the end of the year in a contract position. "He told us he would get back to us," she says. In the meantime he continued to work on the project.

Finally, she says, "We asked for a web meeting to discuss his work. A day would go by and he'd write back with a strange reason for not responding. Saying his kids were on the computer using too much bandwidth. He'd promise to call, then didn't. He built a track record of not following through."

And that led the employer to conclude that he'd be that way on the job, too. He was soon out of the running.

This hit home with me recently when I hired a temporary worker for a program I was doing in Atlanta. I put out a call for what I needed—a musician. Several musicians I contacted took up to three weeks to respond. Others never bothered to get back to me at all. Out of all the qualified musicians I had contact with, I ended up choosing the person I did because he acted like he wanted the job and for all the right reasons.

Yes, his credentials were impressive. He plays harp, cello, and organ and composes music. He has performed with orchestras across the United States and Europe. As for education, he has a Master of Music degree from St. Louis Conservatory (now part of Washington University) and he's studied at the University of Georgia toward his doctoral degree.

But it didn't matter to me where he got his degree or which orchestras he had performed with. When it came down to deciding between him and a violinist and guitarist with equally fine credentials that I discovered, there was no contest.

How he *acted* and therefore *seemed* clinched the deal.

From the first e-mail he sent in response to my e-mail, he acted like a professional who cared about his work and my project and was eager to learn more.

In that first e-mail, I got a feel for him just by the way he communicated in his writing. He wrote complete, coherent sentences.

I could tell he was considerate and approached things in a thoughtful manner. He expressed his appreciation to be considered for the project. He was interested in my project and explained why. He wrote an entire paragraph on that. He read my e-mail thoroughly and responded to every point.

The more we talked and communicated, the more I could tell he understood what I needed.

Over the next few weeks, he responded to my follow-up e-mails. He didn't leave me wondering for weeks if I didn't hear back. Instead, he let me know that he wouldn't be able to talk until late December because of the holiday season—his busy time of year. He was flexible about the scope of the project. When it came to following up with more information, he did everything he said he would. I could tell by his questions that details mattered as much to him as they do to me.

He proved to me I could count on him, that I could trust him to show up with not only the skills I needed, but the type of character and commitment the job called for. How did I conclude that? He was interested and responsive.

Don't

- Wait until tomorrow to respond to an employer.

- Ask about hours, pay, and benefits early in the conversation.

- Ignore people who contact you.

Employers will conclude . . .

- You aren't interested in the position.

- You don't take the lead or follow through.

- You aren't reliable.

- You aren't particularly motivated.

- You aren't a good communicator.

Do

- Respond to an employer quickly.

- Be curious and ask questions that will help you understand the employer's needs and whether you have what it takes.

- Make sure the employer can reach you by sharing your contact information and best times to reach you.

- Follow up quickly to other employer requests.

#8: Don't Fixate on What You Lack

Everyone has issues.

You may have a college degree in the "wrong" field. Or no degree. Perhaps you've had six jobs in 10 years. Or you haven't worked in two years, never worked outside the home, or have no experience beyond an internship.

Every single person has a not-so-perfect circumstance—by choice or not—or things they lack or wish were different. But it doesn't have to turn into the thing that clouds or dooms your success in a job hunt.

I understand why you might think otherwise. Remember that back in Chapter 1, we talked about how employers, being the human beings they are, do what psychologists call "negative filtering." This means they focus on the negative and fail to pay attention to the positive. Then later we talked about how they can't help themselves; it's just natural to immediately look for something that's wrong (and employers do this in part to make their selection process more efficient).

Since you too are human, that's what you do as well—have a tendency to focus on what's wrong or what you lack. This is especially true when you're stressed. But you might do it because, as psychotherapist and author Jonathan Alpert says, "People don't like to set themselves up for disappointment." So, by "focusing on what they think they lack, they feel they have a more accurate view and won't naively approach a situation that they feel is doomed for failure."

Without getting into a lot of psychology, let's just say that people are wired this way.

With the employer's inclination to be on the alert for what's faulty and your leanings toward dwelling on your deficits, you're headed toward conversations and interviews that will be short and not so sweet.

So what's a wired-to-look-for-the-worst person to do?

Deal with your own head first. We'll get to the employer's head in a minute.

Your real liability is believing that an employer will see you as flawed—similar to the "I'm too old" thinking. I've seen it a thousand times.

But you say, "What about the fact that I stayed at home for five years?"

Well, what about it? You can't change it. You're not flawed because of it. But if you think you are, so will they.

What about the fact that you took off two years to try your hand at organic farming in Wisconsin?

One employer will think it's a life-enhancing experience and that you're caring and adventurous. Another might think, "How dumb was that?"—especially when you've got an MBA from Harvard.

What about the fact that you worked for Lowe's your first two years after graduation?

Does that make you hopelessly and forever flawed? Not so fast.

It could mean you had a great experience where you learned about inventory management, operations, and customer relations—an experience that has helped prepare you for this job. And that's exactly what you can say. More on that coming up.

You can't make and then regret life decisions because it might look bad to some stranger. Your choices and your circumstances have not ruined you. So please stop fixating on what you lack (or worry that employers are) and concentrate on what matters: how to *influence* employers' thinking. In other words, help the employer see that your perceived liability is not an issue.

Of course, it's helpful to anticipate objections and concerns an employer might have. And now that you shifted your focus to influencing the employer, you can do that.

Start by having a well-thought-out explanation as to why your absence from the workplace *isn't* an issue. Here's where my "Help Them Get Over It" Formula comes in.

MY "HELP THEM GET OVER IT" FORMULA

Step 1: Expect employers to have issues.
They've got a picture in their head of an ideal candidate. With their tendency to zero in on what you lack, they'll be looking for reasons to eliminate you. Before talking to an employer, think through what the ideal candidate looks like and reasons the employer might find you "deficient." Write them out.

Step 2: Calm the air.
It feels good when someone agrees with you. So when you're in an interview on the phone or in person and you sense apprehension or hear the slightest inkling—"I'm not sure you have the right educational background"—agree. Say something like, "I can understand why you might feel that way." This lowers tension and opens up the conversation.

Step 3: Trot out your evidence to the contrary.

Now help the employer see why the concern needn't be a concern at all. You've thought through these reasons in Step 1, so you're not going to freeze up. Instead you calmly explain, "I did get my degree in English, which has been quite helpful in (whatever way). Since then, I've taken continuing education classes in (whatever those are). My last job included four years handling such-and-such, so I have firsthand experience with the kind of issues this job addresses. Having done that, I also learned this-and-that about myself . . . "

Step 4: Mosey on back to discuss what else you offer.

Now that you've gotten over that hump, gently guide the interviewer back to your strengths and other value: "Speaking of project management, I'm in the process of completing my Project Management certification . . . "

And while we're on the topic of experience and "right" education, let me remind you of what we discussed way back at the beginning—something employers have told me over and over again: You can have all the "right" experience, skills, and knowledge but not get past a phone screening or a first interview because of how else you *seem*.

But what if you lack experience or don't have the "right" degree?

"Anyone can learn," says Zuckerman. He adds that he's totally open "if you have a degree in history and are curious and excited about my company, the job, and what we do. I'd rather have someone who's ambitious and excited any day than somebody with experience. Any day!"

"If it's down to two people and one is very experienced but the other is personable, smart, engaging, thinks on their feet but needs more training, the second person would definitely be the top contender," a marketing director at a business school told me. "Demonstrating you can tackle challenges quickly and having the right customer service attitude is more important."

When it comes to choosing between experience and attitude, *every* employer told me the same thing: Attitude wins every time.

You may not be perfect in all ways. But who is? How you look at your circumstance and then deal with it will have more influence on employers. It's a matter of showing them how you "seem."

Don't

▫ Dwell on what's wrong with you and conclude you're flawed.

Employers will conclude . . .

▫ You're not confident.

▫ You're defensive.

Do

▫ Think through logical explanations for where you have been and the various choices you've made in your career or in preparing for your career.

▫ Think through:

  – the characteristics the ideal candidate would have for this job

  – what an employer might be afraid you won't have

  – any preconceived notions an employer might have about you based on your background or situation

▫ Gracefully help the employer see there is nothing to worry about.

#9: Don't Crank Out Letters Like an Assembly Line

Of all the illogical thinking that goes on in a job search, this one is up at the top of the list: *The more jobs I apply for, the more likely one will pan out.*

Believe that and here's what you'll do:

◻ Crank out cover letters to hundreds of employers and apply for openings you're not qualified for.

Not a good way to spend your time.

Remember that in Chapter 1 Eric Zuckerman talked about hearing from mortgage brokers who apply for designer jobs at his company? If you were to send him an e-mail or letter with your resume for the opening of a designer (which you are not) and write, "I am applying for the position of designer," followed by a few points about your experience as a financial planner (which you have been for 12 years), it wouldn't fly.

Obviously you're neither qualified nor particularly interested in the job of designer; you are just sending your resume to any opening you trip upon. If employers want people who are excited and passionate about the job and industry (#5 on their list), why would they give you the time of day?

◻ Crank out loads of impersonal letters with no reference to the job you're applying for that say things like these (which are for real):

"Here is my resume for consideration."

"I'm applying for the open position."

"Saw your ad on craigs I've attached my resume thanks."

Do I need to explain what kind of reception that will get? Not a welcoming one, I assure you.

- □ Crank out so many letters you get careless.

  A couple of examples courtesy of Rob Basso and Eric Zuckerman:

  – Cover letters written to the wrong company.

  – E-mails saying, "Thanks for the opportunity to apply for your operations manager job" when the job was for a sales position.

  Oops.

  The same goes for your resume.

  And when you're trying to connect with someone on a professional networking site such as LinkedIn, you need to personalize that communication as well. This is especially key when you're approaching someone you don't know through LinkedIn's InMail, which is just like sending an e-mail to someone.

So that's what happens when you're trying to see how many letters you can crank out in a day. All because you think that finding your next position is a numbers game.

It's not. It's about connecting effectively with a live person. As Zuckerman puts it, this kind of carelessness "shows you don't give a damn."

Don't

- □ Apply for jobs that require very specific expertise when the fact is you're completely unqualified for them and have no interest or background in the field.

- □ Send out e-mails and letters that mention the wrong job.

- Send impersonal cover letters, e-mails, and LinkedIn messages.

- Rush off your response to an employer.

Employers will conclude . . .

- You're just looking for a paycheck.

- You don't give a darn.

- You don't value their time.

- You don't pay attention to detail.

- You don't take pride in yourself and your work.

- You're sending cover letters to everybody under the sun and don't give a hoot about their company.

- You may not be qualified since it's not clear what position you are applying for.

Do

- Find out what jobs your target companies may have that fit your expertise.

- Customize every cover letter for the particular job.

- Customize every letter to a company—even if you aren't applying for a particular job.

- Triple-check for factual and typographical errors.

#10: Don't Act Desperate

My dog has perfected the desperate look. He flattens his ears and hunches over slightly with his head lowered and pitched forward.

His pleading eyes meet mine. It always works. I give him whatever he wants. But for you—in a job hunt—desperation is not a good thing. It will have the opposite effect and scare employers away.

It's a bad sign "when people start talking about why they need this job so bad," says Dianne Durkin.

"They'll say, 'I've got a sick mother. We don't have medical coverage,' or 'I've got two new kids.' Or 'My husband lost his job and isn't making enough money like he used to,' or 'We're trying to put our kids through college.'"

What does it tell her? "These people are not really looking for a career position or to grow with our company."

It may also seem like a good idea to tell the employer, "I can do anything." But you will appear to be desperate. It shows you haven't thought about where you can make a difference, while others competing for the same job have.

Desperation also comes across when someone is "overeager to say the right things," says Rob Basso. It's a big old red flag, he says.

"They're not talking about solving any problems for us. They come off as extremely nervous. And they're talking about their past skills and near desperation to get a job," he says.

Then there are those who are just blatantly desperate. Take the cabdriver featured in a *New York Times* article in 2011. In the hopes of landing a hedge-fund position, he placed a laminated piece of paper in his cab that read: "Ask to see my resume. You won't be sorry!"

He said he figured "the best way to market myself was to be driving around town with a sign that said, 'Hey, help me! I need a job!'"

Don't

- Say you can do anything.

- Say you need the job for reasons such as medical coverage or to pay your mother-in-law's nursing home bills.

- Focus on what you need.

Employers will conclude . . .

- You aren't skilled to do the job.

- You don't know yourself.

- You only care about the paycheck, not the job.

Do

- Think through why you are qualified for the job and whether you'd enjoy doing the job, and show employers why they would like working with you.

- Talk specifically about how your qualifications match the employer's needs.

#11: Don't Think It's Over When the Interview Ends

Whew. You made it through the interview. And now it's on to the next step. Yes, there is always a next step. It's also an opportunity to strengthen your connection, help the employer get a sense of your value, and rustle up more show-stopping evidence to outshine the competition.

Rarely, if ever, do employers decide right on the spot and at their very first interview to offer you the job. There usually are second or third interviews, and sometimes more. They have to talk it over with others. They may be meeting more applicants.

As you're driving away from the interview, instead of texting (you should never do this while driving) or talking on your cell phone (it's best not to do that while driving either), here's what you should be thinking about:

What can I do to reinforce the good impression I made? How do I make sure they don't forget me? What needs to happen to move this forward?

Yes, that means communicating more.

That first communication comes in the form of a personal thank-you letter—preferably to everyone you met. Yes, I must stubbornly insist that every human you meet in a job hunt gets a sincere, personal thank-you letter. I don't care if you're applying for an entry-level job or an executive role; if you want to be a contender, you must type and send as soon as humanly possible—within 24 hours—a well-written, error-free business letter or e-mail that thanks everyone for their time and reminds them why you stand out above all others.

This type of letter will *not* do:

> "Dear Mr. Casey: Thank you very much for your time and interest in me for this position. I look forward to hearing back from you."

You think that will keep him up at night remembering how special you are?

This is your chance to remind everyone you met of how you can be of immediate value and how interested you are in the position—two good reasons to hire you. What type of letter will do that?

After the initial niceties ("Thank you for the opportunity to meet . . ."), keep them intrigued with something like this: "I've been thinking about our conversation regarding the international market. Here are a few thoughts on how I might approach this." Then tell them what those thoughts are.

What did you learn in your conversation? Use it. Summarize the types of things you'd see yourself addressing in the job:

> "After talking, I gained a good understanding of your company's goals. Two areas that seem to need imme-

diate attention are the establishment and training of a new sales force. I have successfully recruited, hired, trained, and managed professional sales teams for two companies that were expanding into the international market. In both instances, the companies were selling their services to Brazil, China, and India and achieved record sales and earnings within one year."

One manager who works for a university that employs over 14,000 people told me she is particularly impressed with someone who takes the time to thank *every* person involved in the interview.

"This shows attention to detail and that they really care and understand that all of these people took time out of the day to meet. It shows great etiquette and professionalism," she says.

What did I tell you? Yes, it's work. And well worth it.

Rob Basso says he has "noticed an alarming drop-off in follow-up, especially from the younger generation. I do expect an e-mail after the interview, recapping their strong points and thanking me for my time."

He says it not only "reaffirms their genuine interest for the job," but guess what? It's also one of the most crucial times to show what kind of worker you'd be. As he points out, "It demonstrates writing and follow-up skills."

It's so important that, "If there's a candidate I'm interested in and I do not receive a follow-up note or call, it definitely weighs against them," he says.

Michael Zwick says the lack of a thank-you letter or e-mail is a deal breaker for him. It not only shows a lack of social graces, but "the failure to send one indicates that the person does not want the job enough. I don't want anyone who doesn't want to be here," he says.

A business owner who had just interviewed a potential account executive for his company told me that what would happen next was dependent on the person he had interviewed. So, he was watching closely to see if the applicant demonstrated the kinds of skills the job demands.

"We'll see what he does next," the employer says. "Will he follow up? Will he write a great thank-you note? If I never hear a word from him, that tells me a lot about what kind of account executive he'd be. Not a very good one."

A badly written thank-you note can also hurt you. Eric Zuckerman interviewed a woman whom he "found very interesting." Then she sent a thank-you note.

"It looked like it was written by a child. My name was spelled wrong and there were errors throughout the entire thing. Why would I bring in someone like that when the job requires such attention to detail?"

Along with or in your next follow-up, you can also send a proposal based on what you discussed. This shows self-initiative (#7 on the list). This doesn't have to be elaborate. I'm not suggesting you spend hours developing detailed marketing plans, competitive analyses, or specific strategies and budgets. That's something you get paid to do.

I'm talking about a proposal that outlines specific problems the position would address. Think of it as a description of the company's objectives and a few sentences explaining how you would contribute. Here's an example.

Sample Section from a Proposal You'd Send After an Interview

Objective: *Better utilize production operations and distribution networks of company subsidiaries.*

How I will contribute: *Develop licensing agreements with other companies in this industry that will result in built-in promotion of company name and products and strengthen customer loyalty.*

Remember: You want to help the employer see that you have the traits, characteristics, and skills the company is looking for. That includes self-initiative; ability to communicate; clear, critical thinking; professionalism; and excitement about the job and industry. Your thank-you note and follow-up give you the chance to do that after an interview. Make the most of it.

Don't

- Sit around wondering when you'll hear back from the employer.

- Write the same "Thanks for your time, I look forward to hearing back from you" thank-you letter to everyone.

Employers will conclude . . .

- You don't follow up.

- You're not that interested in the job.

- You were raised by wolves (and therefore don't have proper etiquette).

Do

- Within 24 hours after your interview, write a sincere, personalized, error-free thank-you letter to everyone you met, reminding them how you can be of immediate value.

#12: Don't Be Uptight and Don't Try to Be Perfect

Have you noticed how you can always spot a job interview taking place over a meal in a restaurant? The hopeful employee is all suited up in navy or black. He's sitting upright in his chair. His arms are stiff as boards and each hand faces palm down, gripping his thighs.

Honestly, if only people could relax a little. It would be much less stressful and so much more productive for the equally apprehensive employer sitting on the other side of the table.

For starters, it would help if you could stop thinking of an interview as a "sell job." It would take a lot of pressure off you. You know how it is. In the back of your head you're thinking, "I have to make them want me, and I'd better not do anything to blow that." Before you know it, you're worrying.

It would work out much better if you could approach the interview as a conversation. Then you'd just be, well, conversing. Not selling anything. Back and forth you'd go. It would sound something like this:

> **Employer:** "So, Julietta, I see you were instrumental in generating income for your radio station. How did you do that?"

> **Julietta:** "Well, first, I planned and executed an expansion of our facility that included total refurbishing of three recording studios. I was able to secure capital improvement funds of over $100 million for technical enhancements. That included overnight automation, a multi-track recording console, and digital audio distribution. Then I spearheaded the marketing of our facilities through an aggressive direct mail and public relations campaign. You did something similar here two years ago, right?"

See how that reminded Julietta of something? (Plus, it showed she did her research.) So then she asked a question. Then the employer responded. Which took the conversation to another level and another issue. And without thinking too much, they had a nice rhythm going. A real conversation.

At the end, everyone felt it went well.

Sure, you still have to be on your toes and not say anything stupid. But what a load you've taken off yourself. And how much more interesting (dare I say enjoyable?) the interview is.

But when you're uptight and trying to be nearly perfect, you create all kinds of issues.

One employer at a university told me she scheduled a face-to-face interview with a woman who sounded like a strong candidate on the phone.

But in person, "She was extremely nervous," the employer says.

"Her voiced quivered. Her neck flushed. I wasn't sure if it was shyness or nervousness. But overall she was very rigid. It was as if she was 'overly professional.' She was stiff. She kept trying to be perfect." And things just got worse.

When the employer asked her to describe a time she made a mistake, what she learned, and how she resolved it, the candidate smiled and said, "I never make mistakes. I'm just perfect, I guess."

Then, the employer says, "there was this nervous laughter. Partly, she was making a joke, but she didn't follow up by really answering the question. I could tell it was important to her to make a good impression. But it was a detriment. She was almost deferential to me, treating me so much like the authority figure she was trying to impress. I wanted to have a conversation."

So how did all this make the candidate *seem* to this employer?

"Like she lacked maturity and professionalism and the skills I needed. I need someone who can think quickly on their feet and who's willing to take responsibility for her mistakes. She wasn't self-aware enough. Based on her demeanor, I felt she might need to be micromanaged."

Not trying to be perfect—in fact, even failing—can be a good thing.

Kyle Zimmer, president and CEO of First Book, told the *New York Times* Corner Office columnist (May 26, 2012) that when she interviews a candidate, she asks, "Have you ever started anything? From the time you were little, did you invent anything? An organization? Did you start a club?"

Then she asks: "What was the hardest part of that? What about failure?" She adds that, "if you're pushing in whatever you're doing, you're going to fail way more than you succeed." So she wants to hear how candidates talk about failure. Do they blame others? What would they do differently? Her company sees trying, giving it your best shot, but still crashing as an "honorable step." It gives Zimmer insight into the kind of person a candidate is.

Overly formal language just doesn't work either. It's not how people really act. "We want to hire real people, not robots," says Chris Hicken, vice president at UserTesting.com.

The other thing uptight candidates do is give yes and no answers, which doesn't make for particularly stimulating conversation.

Eric Zuckerman really dislikes that. "Be engaged!" he told me, with such emphasis it truly deserves an exclamation mark. "If I'm talking about our company and the job and you like what you're hearing, don't just say 'this sounds great.' Have a conversation."

The university employer concurs. She says the Nervous Nelly candidate "would just respond politely to my questions. She didn't elaborate. I felt like I had to pull things out of her."

Equally ineffective are people (especially younger folks) who respond to everything—no matter what you're talking about— with these "Wow!" equivalents: "Yeah, absolutely!" "Awesome!" "Sweet!" "Totally!"

These kinds of Twitter-like responses make it hard to gauge what you think. You need to expand your responses to be taken seriously and to have a meaningful conversation. (More on this in Chapter 4.)

Remember Joe Cheung, director of recruiting for Yammer, an

enterprise software firm in San Francisco? He says he knows a creative, insightful would-be employee who wants to add value to the company on sight because in the interview the candidate "will ask a lot of questions and be more inquisitive about the organization and its culture." That's one of the things you do when you're engaged in the conversation.

Given that you don't yet know if the job is even right for you, holding a conversation also puts you in a better position to evaluate whether this could be a match made in heaven.

When the two of you—or more—are truly conversing, you're getting at what matters most: understanding who the other one is.

I like what Bobbi Brown, founder of Bobbi Brown Cosmetics, said in a *New York Times* article (January 23, 2010). Asked what she is looking for when holding an interview with someone, she said, "I don't think about interviewing them for work. I first try to understand who they are as people."

Yes, you will prepare well for the interview. You'll think through the questions and your responses and then always show yourself in the best possible light.

But an interview is not an inquisition. You don't have to sell yourself. Just be yourself and let the conversation do the selling for you.

Don't

- Turn the interview into a "sell job."

- Try to be perfect.

- Be overly formal.

- Respond to everything simply with "That's great!" "Wow!" "Totally!" or "Awesome!"

Employers will conclude . . .

◘ You are immature.

◘ You aren't a very effective communicator.

◘ You can't handle yourself well in stressful situations.

◘ You don't have much to offer.

◘ You're not authentic.

Do

◘ View the interview as a conversation.

◘ Go with the flow.

◘ Converse and respond so you can get to know each other.

#13: Don't Be Too Casual

"Hey man." That's what one young man kept saying to Eric Zuckerman during their interview.

You might imagine that displeased Zuckerman a tad.

"I don't expect him to say, 'Sir this and that,' but there's way too much informality," says Zuckerman. "You just don't meet people for the first time and call them 'dude' or 'man.'" Especially in a job interview.

You'll stand out all right. And not in a good way.

You can give the impression that you're just too informal in other ways too—the clothes on your body (we'll discuss this in Chapter 5) and things that you insist on not removing from your ears. Take the man who entered an interview with iPod earphones. "Not a great first impression during the handshake," says Kevin Sheridan, senior vice president of HR Optimization at Avatar HR Solutions, a consulting firm.

You'd think they'd know better, but even C-level executives (CEOs, COOs, and CFOs) can act too casual. Just ask Charley Polachi, cofounder and partner at executive search firm Polachi. He works with folks making over $200,000 and cites examples that include execs who use an iPhone or BlackBerry *during* an interview, spew profanity, and trash their current employer. Some even share confidential company information.

This casual, informal way of talking and treating information and people during the interview troubles many employers. Which makes you wonder—why would anyone do that? Is it to get someone to like you?

"People seem to want you to accept them for who they are. But no one is asking you to change who you are or be someone you're not," says Zuckerman.

What people seem to forget is that, "An interview is not everyday life. It's a unique experience. And how you're acting here trying to represent yourself makes me wonder how you'll act when you're comfortable," says Zuckerman.

And that makes him also wonder how you'd act if you worked for him, emphasizing that, "When you're an employee you're a representative of that company. Everything you do speaks to the bigger picture of the company."

As Polachi says, "I am in the 'good fit' business, not the 'good guy/gal' business. I want to be sure these candidates fit with my client and the task that needs to be done."

The more you communicate with someone, the more tempting it is to let your hair down. Especially in e-mail. The language you use will tend to get friendlier. Before you know it, you're addressing people with "Hey" this and "Hey" that. Don't.

Some employers say the acceptance—or not—of such informality depends on the company. "Managers at client-facing companies where senior people must meet with senior clients are more concerned about casual presentation than managers at start-ups, IT, media, or technology-driven companies where employees are from Gen Y or are millennial," says Sheridan.

Others say, "Nothing doing. Industry and age are irrelevant." And yes, the employers who say this are in their early 30s. They work in technology. In California even. Yet they are on the prowl for people who know how to conduct themselves in a business situation. They're assessing it in a job interview. Which is, of course, a business meeting.

Among the 500 managers polled by the Society for Human Resource Management, 65 percent said it was "somewhat of a problem" and 18 percent said it was a deal breaker when an applicant is overly casual and acts as if he or she is talking to friends.

The same goes for your writing. I'll talk in more detail about that in the next chapter.

If you're trying to stand out, "it's your professionalism that will do it," says Zuckerman. "It tells me you're taking this seriously."

Don't

- Get too casual with employers, addressing them informally and treating them like you're old buddies.

- Share company secrets or use profanity.

Employers will conclude . . .

- You don't know how to conduct yourself like a professional.

- You won't treat others with respect.

- Your judgment is questionable.

◻ If you're this way in an interview, you'll act like this at work.

◻ You're not a good "fit."

Do

◻ Treat the interview like a business meeting.

#14: Don't Ignore or Fabricate References

Just because you shared a cubicle wall with Joe Maplestone back in 2007 and went to a cookout at his house once doesn't mean he'll be a cheerleader for you and your career. It's been so long since you worked together, he may not even remember you. Who knows, he may not have been that keen on you in the first place.

And just because Buffy Woodbutton agreed to be your reference back when you were looking for your first job out of college doesn't mean she'd be your reference 10 years later.

References need tending to. You're asking people to vouch for you. If you want someone to speak highly of you, that person needs to feel good about you. You can't ignore prospective references for years and then expect them to hop to it.

That tending to includes making sure they will share the kind of information that will help you, not hurt you.

Years ago a company owner told me he was looking for a salesperson. Before flying an applicant into town for an interview, he checked her references.

When he called one of them, the reference said, "She's a horrible person!" and went on to share more details about the applicant's bad character. It turns out the applicant had an affair with the reference's husband.

Also, make sure someone is actually willing to *be* your reference. I once got a phone call from someone I had known professionally but not well, who told me to expect a call from a company. "I used you as a reference," he told me. He had never asked me if I'd be one.

He didn't know that I had found out months before that he had been fired from his previous job for lying. I would not have agreed to be his reference.

Once someone says, "Yes, I'd be happy to be a reference," you're still not done. How well does the person know you and your current work? Will he or she remember why you're so great? Yes, you need to update references on your background, qualifications, and your present career objective.

So send each reference a new resume. Set a time to talk so you can explain why you're looking for a new job. Remind your references of the successful projects or programs you worked on together. If you know, tell them which companies may be calling. Then follow up to thank each reference after a company has called.

Although it's important to provide names of people who can vouch for you, remember this: The worst thing is to make up references.

Allan Young, CEO of ShelfGenie, told me about one such candidate whose references didn't check out. Young says the applicant gave him three references, but "after multiple attempts, we couldn't get ahold of two of them and the third reference said, 'Yes, I know him but he never worked for me.' We assumed the references were a fabrication."

So much for that person.

Treat your references with care. They are doing you a favor. I once heard a CEO of a technology company tell job hunters that you should "have references send in available time slots for when they are available."

Really?

Your references don't work for you. If and when an employer asks for your references, you can let those people know they will be hearing from the company. They'll work it out from there.

When should you provide your references to prospective employers? When they ask for them. Employers who are really thorough will check out your references before they even meet you. But they will tell you when they want them. Have the names and titles of four to six people you've worked with or worked for, along with their contact information, lined up, neatly typed, and ready to go. And take a copy with you when you interview, in case you're asked for your references then.

Don't

- Make up references.

- Give out names of people as references if you haven't asked them first.

- Expect people you haven't kept in touch with to remember why you're so wonderful.

Employers will conclude . . .

- You're dishonest.

- You've got something to hide.

Do

- Keep your references up-to-date.

- Thank them and follow up.

- Pick people who know you and your work ethic, and why you would be someone an employer would want to hire.

#15: Don't Ruin Your Rep on Social Media

One of the best things to come along that can really help your career is the Internet and all it offers in terms of information and ways to connect with others.

One of the worst things to come along that can really hurt your career is the Internet and all it offers in terms of information and ways to connect with others.

It all depends on how you use it.

The thing is, you're not the only one taking advantage of all the Internet has to offer. Employers are using it to check *you* out.

The exact number of employers who use social media to investigate prospective employees is up for debate. Some surveys say as many as 91 percent of recruiters and managers look at social media when hiring.

Companies are obligated to find as much information as possible about a potential candidate. But unless a company discourages its hiring managers from delving into someone's online persona (it's unclear whether it's legal to use sites like Facebook when it comes to hiring), why wouldn't they? The Internet is filled with all kinds of juicy clues about you. And you're providing it free of charge.

According to an April 2012 CareerBuilder survey of approximately 2,300 hiring managers and human resource professionals, nearly 40 percent use social networks to research potential job candidates. Of that number, 65 percent use Facebook to glean information about you, 63 percent use LinkedIn, and 16 percent use Twitter.

What are they hoping to find? Clues about character and personality—the very things we've been talking about since Chapter 1.

Specifically, 65 percent of those surveyed said they want to see if you present yourself professionally. Fifty-one percent want to see if you're a good fit for their culture. Forty-five percent want to learn more about your qualifications.

Thirty-four percent who research candidates through social media said they found information that caused them *not* to hire someone. My hunch is that it's higher. What did they see that they didn't like?

Does how you want to seem *match up with how you present yourself online?*

The worst offender was provocative or inappropriate photographs. Information about the person drinking or using drugs came in second. From there it was poor communication skills, badmouthing previous employers, discriminatory comments related to race, gender, or religion, and lying about qualifications.

If you do get nixed because of something prospective employers saw online, are they going to tell you that's why they turned you down? Most likely not. But what a gold mine for employers—much better than any traditional personality test. And if you think there's nothing to that statement, think again.

A 2012 study from Northern Illinois University, the University of Evansville, and Auburn University systematically examined the validity of using Facebook to help make hiring decisions. The results, published in the *Journal of Applied Social Psychology*, showed it took about 10 minutes for someone to go through a Facebook profile and predict how the person would perform on the job.

Here's how the researchers reached that conclusion. First they asked human resource specialists to spend 10 minutes reviewing Facebook profiles that included photos, wall posts, comments, educational background, and hobbies of employed college students. Then the HR specialists were asked personality-related questions such as "Is this person dependable?" "How emotionally stable is this person?"

Six months later, the researchers compared the students' job performance reviews, as provided by their supervisors, with the Facebook ratings. They found a high correlation between the perceptions garnered from the Facebook profiles and the students' actual performance for traits like conscientiousness, agreeability, and intellectual curiosity.

What did this tell the researchers? That Facebook is a pretty reliable job-screening tool.

It's also interesting that among the employers in the Career-Builder survey, nearly 30 percent said they found something on social media sites that caused them to *hire* a person. In other words, what they saw gave the job seeker an advantage.

The "something" they found was content that conveyed a professional image or showed that the person was well-rounded, had great communication skills, and was creative. In some cases, other people had posted good references about the job applicant.

It's a matter of managing your public face. You can use social media to establish your expertise and build your professional reputation—but you have to decide that you're going to use it for professional purposes. This will guide you not just in what to say, but in where to post your comments.

If you decide to use social media for professional purposes and you plan to post comments on blogs and other places, choose those that educate as opposed to those that entertain. As one CEO told me, you can be seen as a resource or a rebel. Think about which one your next employer will value more.

Headhunters and CEOs are always looking for creative people, and they do so online. That means you must be on your toes. One information technology executive told me he looks in all kinds of places for innovative thinking, and therefore, "Remember to dot your i's and cross your t's—we are watching."

Use Twitter Wisely

Because of its format, some social media can be more damaging than others. Take the career of Richard Grenell, who was hired in April 2012 by presidential candidate Mitt Romney to be his full-time spokesperson on national security matters. Grenell and his Twitter comments had gained a reputation for telling it like it is. So when his appointment was announced, "his tweets took on world-historical importance," wrote David Weigel in Slate (April 23, 2012).

"In a typical week, Richard Grenell might have tweeted 100 times and started 100 arguments," he wrote. When he was hired and his tweets became such a news item, he scrubbed away over 800 of them.

"Grenell's micro-blogging history had shrunk from 7,577 tweets to 6,759 tweets. This was a massacre—800-odd tweets slaughtered for the cause of Not Embarrassing Romney," wrote Weigel. Grenell also took down his personal website and apologized "for 'any hurt' caused by his 140-character barbs and crack-'em-ups."

Quoting journalist Jonathan Rauch, who is somewhat familiar with Grenell, Weigel said, "Grenell's problem reveals 'what an embarrassing waste of time Twitter is. It's not a medium for adults—it practically begs you to be short, snarky and stupid—and foreign-policy spokesman is a grown-up job.'"

Twitter can be a decent tool to enhance your reputation. Just use it wisely.

Don't

- Post inappropriate photos.

- Bad-mouth employers.

- Make discriminatory comments related to race, gender, or religion.

- Lie about your qualifications.

Employers will conclude . . .

- You won't handle yourself professionally at work.

- You don't fit their culture.

- You're a poor communicator.

- You're immature.

Do

- Decide if you're going to use social media for professional purposes, to guide you in what to say and where.

- Post content that shows you're social, comfortable with others, curious, well-rounded, and have a sense of humor.

- Look for places to establish your expertise and build your reputation, and that establish you as a resource in your field.

These Go Without Saying (Or Do They?)

These may seem obvious. Then again, maybe not. Here are a few more Don'ts that may or may not be obvious:

- *Don't cheat on tests or react negatively while taking them.* Tests can screen for intelligence (your capacity to acquire and apply knowledge), skills (what you can already do), aptitude (your capacity to learn other skills), interests (what you'll most likely enjoy doing), and attitude (how you tend to act or approach things), as well as how you tend to influence others and how you think. And maybe more.

You can never know for sure whether they're doing it, but some of the people who administer the tests also record how applicants *act* while taking them. They're observing: Does the person seem frustrated or act exasperated? It's part of the test. That means your reactions to tests and the way a test is configured can be a test in itself.

Common sense test-taking advice to keep in mind: It's not just about the right answer. It's about the right attitude. And Big Brother could be watching for both.

▫ *Don't chew gum or eat.* Chomping on gum is distracting, annoying, and well, if you're not careful, it can fall out of your mouth. Wouldn't that be embarrassing? And if you're offered a beverage in an interview, fine. That's one thing. But to bring your own drink or food to an interview? Never.

Even if you're speaking on the phone, don't chew or eat. The listener can tell.

▫ *Don't be rude or aggressive.* Nowadays, you may be evaluated by a team of people who would work with you. I've known companies that ask the input of their clients before hiring someone, since the applicant would be dealing with them directly. I've also known people who didn't get a job based on the opinion of coworkers, administrative assistants, and board members. Everyone should be treated with care.

> ❝ The best index to a person's character is (a) how he treats people who can't do him any good, and (b) how he treats people who can't fight back."
>
> —Abigail Van Buren

▫ *Don't hold interviews on speakerphones or cell phones.* The best place to have a phone conversation with an employer is in a quiet room behind closed doors on a landline with the phone to your ear. Speakerphones make you sound distant and distracted. Cell phones make you sound muffled and hard to understand. And there's a greater chance of getting disconnected.

❑ *Don't turn on your cell phone in interviews.* What if it rings? Are you going to answer it? Some people do. It's bad enough that it rang. It's even worse to take the call.

Now, let's get into the 15 things you never want to say or talk about.

four

□ □ □ □ □ □ □ □ □ □

15 Things You Should Never Talk About or Say

Before we jump into the 15 things you should never talk about or say, let me point out three operating principles that will help you digest and apply the points in this chapter.

Operating Principles

1. THINK LIKE YOUR AUDIENCE

Your audience, obviously, is an employer. This is the hardest thing to do—think like the employer—because your brain is filled with the things you're thinking about, including being employed and happy and making decent money. You're probably also worried about making sure you don't end up in a dead-end job and about having a life outside of work. Not to mention what you'll have for lunch and whether you'll run into traffic on the way home.

But you can and *must* don your Employer Thinking Cap. Remember what you learned in Chapter 1: The key to success in job hunting, and in creating a less angst-ridden and more successful life in general, is to *start where things are*, not where you think they *should be*. In this case, you need to start where the employers' heads are and understand how they will likely react to what you say.

This might be a good time to revisit exactly what they want and care about. That list (What Employers Look For) is in Chapter 1.

2. MASTER YOUR CONTENT, THEN GO WITH THE FLOW

By content, I mean anything you're planning to share with employers:

- Your professional experience

- Your strengths

- Stories that illustrate your strengths

- Your breadth of knowledge

- How you approach problems

- Why you left your last job and the one before that

- Your reactions to questions about salary, working arrangements, and hours

Contrary to what you may have heard, there is no such thing as a perfect response to any question. There is no exact order in which to line up your words. Mastering your content is not about memorizing or using precise wording. It's about knowing what you want to say and the point you want to make. It's about knowing your content inside and out and being so comfortable with what you want to say that it is second nature.

When you have mastered your content and know it cold, you can have a real conversation and share examples and stories with ease. You can look at what the moment is calling for, pluck out the details you want to share, and go with the flow.

3. GETTING A JOB IS NOT THE OBJECTIVE OF A JOB INTERVIEW

You've heard this one before—the critical, prevailing principle I laid out at the beginning of the last chapter. The one you posted on the wall. It still applies.

Your objective in a job interview is this: *To explore whether the company and the job are right for you and you are right for the company while presenting yourself in the best possible light.* That goes for everything we talk about in this chapter too.

Like the 15 Things You Should Never Do, some of the 15 Things You Should Never Talk About or Say require more explanation than others. They can apply to your correspondence and conversations *before, during,* or *after* an interview. I break them down into two sections: "Don't Talk About" and "Don't Say." Of course, I also discuss what to talk about and say instead.

Now let's focus on specific things you never want to talk about or say.

#1: Don't Talk About Things You Can't Back Up

You're a good team player—so you say. Can you tell me more?

Mmmm, Let me think, you say?

This is not a good sign.

If you're going to make a statement such as "Works well on teams" on your resume or in a cover letter, you'd better know what you mean. The same goes for live conversations.

It might be true. You might be the most supportive, reliable, cooperative, flexible, committed team player on the planet. The question is: Where? How? What exactly did you do that made you so effective? What was the result?

You say you're passionate about this work. OK, tell me more.

Well, let me think, you say.

Really? You have to think about that too? Passion means to have a powerful, compelling emotion or feeling. It implies you have drive, great enthusiasm, fascination. If you have to think about why you're passionate about this work, well, maybe you aren't.

You would be a valuable asset to our group, you say?

Can you share some examples of how you've contributed to these kinds of projects in the past and why that was so terrific?

Silence.

Not being able to provide specific examples of how you contributed to a project and where you've added value is a big misstep—and one that Tonya Lain, regional vice president for Adecco Group, a staffing and recruiting firm, sees over and over.

She describes candidates who can't provide a detailed description of how they fixed a problem or how they went above and beyond the call of duty. "They aren't articulating or demonstrating what they are willing to do to set themselves apart."

One employer told me about such an interview with a candidate for a public relations job. The employer really wanted to understand her skills. She had worked on an awards program for a large company, describing it as "a big success." When he asked her specifically what she did to create such a success, here's how the conversation went:

Employer: "What did you do?"

Candidate: "You know, I let people know about it."

Employer: "How? Did you send out a news release?"

Candidate: "Yes."

Employer: "Who did you send it to?"

Candidate: "Well, you know. News media."

Employer: "What else did you do?"

Candidate: "You know. I worked on it."

Employer: "What did you do?"

Candidate: "I called some people. I sat in on some meetings. It was very successful."

Employer: "What makes you say that?"

Candidate: "Everybody was happy."

Clearly, she had not thought through nor mastered her content.

If you can't explain what you mean, don't say it. But if your claims have merit, make those words come to life. Do so in a way that the employer can digest it: in small, yet complete, enticing bites. Then be prepared to tell more details.

Besides helping employers see your value, you'll be getting to the heart of what every employer is hoping you have:

- The ability to communicate so others can understand what you're talking about

- The ability to consider and analyze data and then summarize it in a way that's relevant to the listener

- The ability to think on your feet

Would it help to have some nifty techniques to show you how to do that?

Here you go.

HOW TO MAKE YOUR CLAIMS COME TO LIFE

1.   Pretend a seven-year-old is sitting in front of you. How would you explain a complicated job or project you were involved in to her? How would you slim down your explanation?

Or think through how to summarize a key accomplishment in two or three sentences.

Let's say, for example, you want to show that you know how to lead others and do it well even in less-than-perfect circumstances. A good example is from this past year, when you led a team of people from four different disciplines who are scattered around three countries. You were able to complete a huge information technology project on time with the help of this team.

So how can you summarize that in a sentence or two in a way that's relevant and clear?

Think simple. Like those good old sentence-diagramming days when you broke sentences into a subject, verb, and direct object, enhanced with adjectives. It might sound something like this: "My team of brilliant engineers, lawyers, and marketing and IT wizards from Europe, Asia, and America met weekly for a month, launching the largest IT implementation project in the company's history in time for the opening of the new facility."

You can elaborate, of course. See where the conversation goes. If the employer says, "How did you do that?" share more detail. Of course, think through the gist of what you'd say.

2.   To explain what you've been doing lately, what you've accomplished, and how your work has made a difference, answer this question: If *USA Today* were writing an article about the past six months of your life, what would the headline say? What would the article discuss?

A sample headline might be this: "James Jupiter Managed Implementation of Largest IT Project in Company History, Adding Over $3MM in Revenues."

If you haven't been contributing to a company in the past six months or more, make the headline about training you've taken to improve yourself, what you've learned as you keep up-to-date in your field, or trends you're tracking that can apply to this job:

"Maria Studies Ways Computer Games Can Train Patients to Care for Themselves as Health-Related Games Take Over 20 Percent Of 'Game Market.'"

GIVE ME SOME PROOF

You can have all the talent in the world, but the employer is taking a big risk by hiring you. They don't want to spend $10,000 to $30,000 to hire and train you, only to learn six months later you were full of hot air. They want proof.

This would be proof that helps them see you are the solution to their problems. Proof that makes them say, "OK, I see how you did that in the past. That's what I want you to do for me."

Most of your competition hasn't taken the time to figure out their proof either. When you do, you'll be *miles* ahead of them. *You will stand out.*

You can come up with proof whether you have loads of experience, have just graduated from school, or have done mostly volunteer or unpaid work. You may think what you do isn't measurable. But everything has a result. Whether you're moving tickets for a theater performance or implementing software that will let a bank support capital markets and private banking, it's about results.

So if you're going to say, "My strengths include the ability to lead others," be ready to cite a juicy example or two of how you've done that. If you don't, when asked, you'll fumble around and say things like "I have a lot of experience leading people to get great results." Do you hear how lame that is?

Or you'll be as inarticulate as that woman in my previous example who tried to explain what she did to create a successful awards problem.

She said: "You know. I worked on it." "Everybody was happy."

It's all well and good to just tell an employer where you excel. But it's not enough. With that kind of response you're asking employers to make a great leap of faith to believe you're fabulous and want to hire you. I assure you, you won't sound so fabulous.

Don't

- Name projects, knowledge, experience, and personal attributes in your letters, resume, online, or in conversations unless you can discuss them in nice, juicy detail.

Employers will conclude . . .

- You can't do the work the job entails.

- You're exaggerating or not being honest about your abilities.

- You don't understand what the work requires.

- You're not an effective communicator.

Do

- Think through your content and specific scenarios to explain what you do and how you do it. For example, if you want to show you've worked on teams, provide details about a successful team project. What was the problem you were solving? How were you a valuable contributor to the project? How did you make a difference?

- Think through the qualities you exhibit. Are you a great team player? Do you speak up and share ideas in a constructive way? Are you known for your ability to consider other points of view? Do you come prepared for meetings with a "what can I do to help us succeed?" approach? Do you look for solutions instead of whom to blame when things go wrong?

▫ Look at everything you claim to be and to have done on your resume, in your cover letters, and when you talk about yourself. Look at the adjectives you use. Can you back them up? Look at the types of projects you say you know how to handle. Can you give examples?

#2: Don't Talk About Bad Bosses and Companies, Ex-Husbands and Wives, and Negative Things in General

You might feel better pouring your heart out about your nightmare boss, others who did you wrong, the depressing economy—even those orange barrels you had to avoid to get to the interview on time. But what it says about you is not for the better.

When it comes to talking negatively about others—in particular past employers—here's what the employer is thinking: "You'll do it to us if you did it to them."

This thinking was aptly demonstrated in a 2012 episode of AMC's *Mad Men*. Ad man Don Draper is having a cocktail with the Dow Corning executive. Draper is hoping to drum up new business for his advertising agency at the American Cancer Society soiree in the mid-1960s that many corporate executives are attending. He's a guest and has just been exalted for writing his "Why I'm Quitting Tobacco" letter in the *New York Times*.

His letter, a full-page ad in the paper, says he's relieved that a long relationship with Lucky Strike is over.

"For over 25 years we devoted ourselves to peddling a product . . . that never improves, that causes illness and makes people unhappy . . . when Lucky Strike moved their business elsewhere,

I realized, here was my chance to be someone who could sleep at night, because I know what I'm selling doesn't kill my customers."

Now here he is having a drink at the Cancer Society event with the Dow Corning exec, who tells him it's a waste of time to introduce him to the other executives. "They love your work," he says, "but they don't like you. They'll never work with you—not after that letter. How could they trust you . . . after the way you bit the hand?"

Draper is stunned as these words sink in. The "You'll Do It to Us If You Did It to Them" Rule apparently never occurred to him.

This is what makes bad-mouthing your present or past employer and others risky business. I don't care what they did. Whether they didn't honor their word to give you a promotion or training you'd need. Or if your boss was a first-class knucklehead.

When you "bite the hand" and go negative in a public way, you're the one the potential employer is now questioning. Your past company may have done you wrong. But you blast the hand that fed you, this employer is wondering what that says about you.

The more public, the worse the fear under the "You'll Do It to Us If You Did It to Them" Rule. The potential employer is thinking: "If we hire him, this might be us he's talking about someday."

As the Dow Corning character points out: How can they trust you?

One employer told me that she purposely asks open-ended questions to get people talking and to get a sense of their disposition.

"I'll say, 'Tell me about your experience at your last company.' If they start heading south talking negative, that's telling. It makes me think that negative perspective will likely be the way they think and act at work too. And I really don't want that type of person infiltrating our workforce."

Others say such a comment makes them wonder: Will this person be a pain in the neck? How long will it be before they get mad at me about something?

Rob Basso of Advantage Payroll Services says when people bash their boss in an interview, "You have to assume they left on bad terms and that they will do the same to you and your company in the future."

I understand the need to vent about the people you work with. Really, I do. They can be a pain. I understand the need to vent about your boss. Half the people who come to me moan about all the stupid things—in their estimation—that their bosses do.

It's not to say that employers don't do things worthy of your wrath. Plenty do. But the past is the past. For your own good, it's best to leave it there before things turn ugly in the interview. In the 2009 Society for Human Resource Management survey, 95 percent of employers said talking negatively about a previous supervisor was somewhat of a problem or a deal breaker; 95 percent also said that talking negatively about a previous job or internship was somewhat of a problem or a deal breaker.

If you did leave your last job under circumstances that were less than good, you need a well-thought-out response that does not reveal dangerous details of a relationship gone sour. So no comments about Neanderthal knucklehead bosses you had to put up with. Steer clear of saying things like the following—which are actual responses:

> "Our company was stupid enough to let our entire department go."

> "The company didn't appreciate me and never listened to my ideas. If it had, this wouldn't have happened."

> "That company only cared about getting rich and didn't give two hoots about loyal, hardworking people."

A better approach: You can chalk up your departure to the economy. And as others before you have had to do, come up with a reasonable explanation using artfully chosen words.

Something simple will do:

> "I worked for the S. J. Mathers Company for the last
> 15 years and enjoyed my position. But like many companies these days, they were hit by the recession and
> downsized the workforce. Unfortunately, my division
> was affected."

I highly recommend you work through any toxic bitterness that can come with such a loss. Complain to someone who's close to you, won't talk back, and will let you go on and on about what made you angry. Let it out until you're sick of hearing yourself complain.

If you don't, you may think you're hiding your anger. But in an interview, employers will hear that tinge of sarcasm when you talk about your former boss. It will make them wonder, "What's up?"

It also helps to realize that a job loss is not a mortal wound. Going through setbacks can help you remake yourself into a new, more valued asset. That's something that people definitely understand these days.

In general, it's not wise to bring up *any* negative information. It's one of the biggest mistakes that Katherine Spencer Lee, senior district president of Robert Half International, sees among job-hunting candidates.

"People complain about the drive to the interview, when that would be their commute if they got the job," she points out. When one person who was interviewing for a senior-level accounting position complained about his drive there, it made her wonder: If she hired him, would he want to stay on the job or look for a new one?

Managers want to hire people they'll enjoy working with, she adds, and negativity isn't an attractive trait.

Even if an interviewer goads you, don't get hooked. Michael, a former television producer and anchor I once interviewed, remembers the job that got away after spilling his guts about his boss. He was in the middle of an interview with the general manager of a television station who asked him why he wanted to change jobs.

"At first, I said simply that I wasn't happy in the old place," he says. Then the manager asked him, "Why?"

"Oh, many things," Michael answered. But the interviewer just sat there and the silence grew.

So Michael added that what he didn't like started at the top—meaning his boss. And he went on from there.

"Never one to hold back in expressing my feelings, I told [him] just how I felt. Bad idea. After I'd said what I thought of my boss, I had a funny tickling in the back of my mind. Something had gone wrong. A change in the atmosphere, from cordial to not-so-cordial."

The next day when Michael was back at work, his boss said, "I understand you talked with YY yesterday. He's a good friend of mine, you know." Oops.

Michael didn't get the new job. And things at work got icy. He was demoted from news director and evening anchor to evening reporter with little to do. "I was out of there within six months. I should have kept my mouth shut," he says.

His advice: "Never talk about other people, especially your current employer, or any former employer for that matter."

Don't

- Offer negative opinions or evaluations of your former or current boss or the way the company does business.

Employers will conclude . . .

- Your attitude isn't good for business or morale.

- You won't fit the company.

Do

- Think through how you'll handle potentially touchy questions about why you left your last company. Stick to facts.

- Work through any resentment and anger you have before you talk to employers.

- Steer clear of negative information and complaining in general.

#3: Don't Talk About Money, Perks, and Other "What Will You Do for Me?" Items

"If the first question someone asks is, 'How much vacation do we get?' the interview is just about over," says Allan Young, CEO of ShelfGenie.

Other turnoffs—especially in the first interview or communication—include these questions: How many hours a week am I expected to work [when it's a salaried position]? Do we get free coffee?

For Rob Basso it's also this one: How many sick days do you offer?

"It drives me crazy," he says—especially when an applicant asks in the first five minutes. Or "'Is there a place I can take a smoke break?' It's hard to overlook a comment like that."

But the "what's-in-it-for-me" question that irks employers most is the one about money. So don't ask, "How much does this job pay?"

There are two main reasons you don't discuss money and other related perks and benefits—that is, until the time is exactly right (which I'll discuss in a minute.)

The first thing is that money is not your priority—or shouldn't be.

Really. Think about it. Would you take any job just for the money? Even if it meant you were so unhappy it made you sick? I've had clients making big bucks who were so unhappy and dispirited they gave it up for peace of mind, time with their family, or to save their marriage.

So, for your own good, let's put money in its proper place. To find anything near satisfaction in the work you do, you have to like what you do, be in a culture and environment that suits you, work for a firm you believe in, and finally, be fairly compensated for your contribution.

By bringing up the subject of money in a first interview or early in the process before the time is right, you make it seem like a priority. For your *own* welfare, your first priority should be the scope of the work, where you do it, and how you'd contribute.

By making money a priority, you are also saying to the employer that what you care about most is "what you can do for me." The company is not in the business of doing something for you. And, as several employers point out, this attitude will put an abrupt end to an interview.

Second, the company may use money as a screening device. The employer may be thinking, Is this person too expensive? Or too cheap (and therefore, underqualified)? If either, the company doesn't want to waste its time. So if you discuss money and let on that you're too expensive or too cheap, you could get weeded out before the employer even knows how terrific you are. And by talking about money too early, you also blow your chances to negotiate later. So, first, you have to *establish your value.*

When is it all right to talk about money? After a company has made you an offer. (Which means you have established your value.)

Yes, the employer may bring up the subject of money before there's an offer. You may be asked what kind of salary you're looking for. That's when a response like this comes in handy:

> "Although money is an important issue, it's not my priority. What matters most to me is to explore whether I can make a difference here. I really don't know enough at this point. It seems like it would make sense to discuss salary once we decide I'm right for the job."

Saying this also reinforces what's most important to the employer—that you're someone who cares about how you'll contribute.

As for people who ask about salary, Basso says, "It tells me they're more fiscally motivated versus interested in the actual job and long-term growth." (These are #5 and #9 on the list in Chapter 1.)

Remember what the director of recruiting at Yammer, Joe Cheung, said about looking for signs that you are the kind of person the company wants to hire? He said such folks *are more inquisitive about his organization and its culture.*

"They ask about what it's like to work at Yammer—not about our salary and perks. Their biggest concern is about whether they can actually add value," says Cheung. (That's #15 on the list).

That's where your head should be too—talking about your skills, knowledge, your passion for this type of work, examples of how you've made a difference, and how you can do that at their company. This is the kind of information that establishes your value.

NO "WHAT CAN YOU DO FOR ME?" DEMANDS

Once you're offered a position, you also need to be careful about wandering into potentially inappropriate demands. There's nothing wrong with exploring options. It all depends on how you handle it. Here's an example of how one job hunter handled it poorly.

The owner of a small business was in the middle of exploring how to bring on her first employee. The candidate had volunteered to work on a project for the company so the employer could test out his work. When the owner asked him his salary expectation, he said, "I'll get back to you." A week later the owner got an e-mail that included a lot more than salary expectations. It was a list of 10 conditions.

First on the list: to be paid for the work he had offered to do free of charge. Second was how he expected to be paid: weekly or bi-weekly, "one pay period in arrears, via locally-sourced bank check or electronic transfer."

Another condition: to be allowed to list the company on his resume as an employer—"with no reference to contracted employment terms."

Also, his job title would include "software development manager," even though he would manage neither any person nor any thing. Other stipulations included being available on-site "for no less than 40 hours per week," excluding national holidays and state election days.

The kicker: He would "receive within 30 days of active contract work a favorable letter of recommendation and similar posting on my LinkedIn account, provided that you are satisfied with my work products."

"All we wanted to know was his rate," says the owner. "But he came back with all these unreasonable conditions. He's asking me to be deceitful by giving him a title and job description for his resume and LinkedIn that would not be representative of what he'd have with our company.

"What if he became a slouch after 30 days when he got what he wanted—to put our company name on his resume? His overall tone was 'I'm using you.'

"I understand there's give and take. But this seemed excessive. He asked me to be complicit in something I don't feel is right."

From your point of view, yes, you can define and share your parameters with potential employers. But not like that.

All he had to do was ask the right questions to better understand the company's expectations.

"Just ask us, 'What kind of commitment and hours does the job require?'" says the owner. Then discuss it and find a solution that works for everyone.

This story didn't work out well for anyone. Just as the company owner was thinking she had a solution for her needs, the candidate's follow-up changed everything.

"Now, we have no intention of hiring him," she says.

Your job-hunting philosophy should be this: Ask not what the company can do for you, but what you can do for the company. With this in the back of your mind, you don't want to be asking self-serving questions in the interview.

If you're interested in a mutually beneficial relationship, the right questions can demonstrate that loud and clear.

These questions include: What are the key responsibilities of the job? What types of problems would I face and be asked to solve? What are your expectations of someone in this role? (For more examples of the right questions, see Chapter 3, #7: Don't Act Blasé, Unresponsive, and Disinterested.)

HOW YOU ASK QUESTIONS IS JUST AS IMPORTANT AS THE QUESTIONS THEMSELVES

For example, you may be dying to know how a company treats its employees. Or whether they trust employees to do the best job possible. How would you discover this?

Many people say they'd simply ask, "How do you treat your workers?"

But an employer would likely wonder why you're asking. Do you have a chip on your shoulder from your last experience? Just what are you expecting?

Getting back to that mutually beneficial relationship, a better question would be, "How do your employees fit into achieving the company's long-term goals?" Or "What is your management philosophy?" "What is the company's leadership style and values?"

Instead of asking, "How do you give raises and promotions?" try "How do you evaluate performance?" The latter implies you are responsible for your growth and don't just feel entitled to a raise and promotion.

I had a client who wanted to make sure the company was progressive in hiring and mentoring women. She planned to ask, "How many women sit on your board or are in senior management?"

I suggested a few tweaks: "How have women progressed at your company?"

Before you ask a question, think about whether it might put someone on the defensive.

Another client told me how well an interview was going until the end, when the interviewer asked, "Do you have any more questions?"

My client, who worked in the same industry the company was in, said: "I noticed your company is not in the circle of people I know. You don't seem to network much. Is that something you want to change?"

She found out later that the question did her in. The interviewer saw it as a criticism, which is not a good way to kick things off with the person who would be your next boss.

If you want to get a sense of the culture (how people communicate and treat each other; overall priorities and attitudes) and how management thinks, try these: "Do you encourage creative input from employees?" "What does it take to be successful here?" "What's your customer service philosophy?" "How important is experimenting and coming up with new ideas?"

Don't

- Ask about salary, benefits, and other self-serving issues before you get an offer.

- Make any demands.

Employers will conclude . . .

- You are difficult to deal with.

- You only care about the money and what you will get.

Do

- Ask questions that will help you understand the company's expectations.

- Artfully dodge questions about salary and then focus the conversation on the job.

- Ask questions to explore how to create a mutually beneficial relationship.

It's not a good sign when you start off the interview asking, 'What are the office hours?' or 'What time do I need to be there?'"

—Tonya Lain, regional vice president, Adecco Group

#4: Don't Talk About TMPI (Too Much Personal Information)

It's understandable that you want to cozy up to your potential new employer. Just don't get too chummy by blabbing about personal problems, your love life, politics, and religion, and issues you'd only share with a close friend.

This includes details about your rocky marriage. Bouts with depression. Hard-luck stories about sick children, pets, and mothers; broken-down cars; or a spouse's bad job situation.

Why would you even want to go there? To create a bond with the employer? Are you hoping to gain sympathy and make someone want to hire you? It has the opposite effect.

I'll remind you what Eric Zuckerman said about that woman who went on and on about her personal issues for 20 minutes during the interview. He concluded: She's outta here.

Besides the wrong attitude and a bad fit, her behavior showed poor judgment and lack of professionalism. He, like most employers, is looking for mature individuals who "understand where to draw the professional line."

When someone can't leave personal issues at the door before they come into work, it makes an employer wonder: Does that person have the necessary maturity?

Another employer told me how the person he was interviewing talked about a trip he and his boyfriend had taken.

"It was totally unrelated to what we were discussing in the job interview," says the employer. "I think he wanted to make sure I knew he was gay. I don't care what his sexual orientation is. But the fact that he brought this up put questions in my head about his judgment that weren't there before. Would he also feel the need to let clients know? Some may not be so open-minded."

Zuckerman recalls an interview with a public relations person in which she "started talking about how she represents clients in the fur industry. I have certain views on this," he says, adding that it's best not to "put anything out there that could be conflicting with someone's beliefs."

As he points out, "An interview is not a therapy session." Nor is it the place to talk about anything but the job at hand and your qualifications to do it.

Remember what we discussed in Chapter 3 about not acting desperate. Even if you're in dire straits, employers aren't going to hire you because of what you *need*. They're going to hire you because of *how well you'll solve their problems*. When you share too much information—especially of a personal nature—you are not seen as someone who can solve their problems but as someone who would *be* a problem if they hired you.

Don't

- Discuss personal information that has nothing to do with your qualifications for the job.

- Talk about politics, religion, or the state of your health.

- Talk about why you need the job. For example: "I really need this job because my husband got laid off and we lost our health insurance and it's putting a strain on my marriage. We're in therapy now. But we've had some knock-down, drag-outs."

Employers will conclude . . .

- Your personal life is such a wreck you may not be dependable.

- You're overly dramatic.

- You lack good judgment and don't know where to draw the professional line.

- You're immature.

Do

- Focus on why you're qualified.

#5: Don't Talk About Irrelevant or Dumb Things That Just Pop into Your Head

These comments come in all shapes and sizes.

Take this response one job hunter told me he made and immediately regretted. When asked why he wanted the job he was interviewing for, he said, "I'm looking for friends."

"I knew the minute I said it, it was the wrong thing to say. It just popped into my head," he says.

Or take the time Eric Zuckerman was interviewing a woman for the position of office manager and he asked her one of those oldie but goody questions: Where do you see yourself in five to ten years?

"I see myself having my own medical practice," she said.

What? he thought. *You want to be a doctor?*

"So what are you doing here?" he asked her.

"By her response, she was telling me this is just a job, not something she cared about. And we want someone who really wants to work here."

A marketing director at a university says the interview with one candidate was going well until the person "took me incredibly by surprise as I was escorting her out. She asked to see the physical space where this job would be. I showed her, but it felt inappropriate. This was our first interview. What did that have to do with the actual job? I'm not looking for perfection. But you need to read your environment and react accordingly. This displayed a lack of good judgment."

And then there's the sharing of irrelevant data. This same employer says, "When I ask someone why they're attracted to the position and they say, 'My family, fiancé, or children live in town,' it gives me pause. I feel they're not necessarily interested in the job as much as relocating."

How do such moments happen?

Sometimes, people are just unaware. Or they don't consider the consequences of their words. Stress can be the culprit. Other times, it's something deeper.

Here's an example of "something deeper" in a new business meeting (which is not unlike a job interview.) A man told me that he was in a meeting with his boss and a potential new client located in a city several hours away. When the potential client brought up the distance between them as a liability, the boss blurted out, "Don't worry, we can get here in 15 minutes in the Sikorsky."

He was referring to state-of-the-art Sikorsky helicopters, which he did not own or have access to.

His response might have been his wishful fantasy to do whatever the client needs, says Deborah Smith-Blackmer, a clinical social worker. And that could be driven by desperation, giving way to fabrication "fueled by an impulse to rescue the situation."

Sometimes, "It's as if we have no filter between our brain and our mouth," says BJ Gallagher, author of *Why Don't I Do the Things I Know Are Good for Me?* (Berkley Trade, 2009).

To be less impulsive, you need to practice—literally practice, says Smith-Blackmer. Slow down, count to five, and give yourself a chance to consider how your comment will sound.

Don't

▫ Blurt out things that just come to you at the moment.

- Share irrelevant data.

- Get too chummy.

Employers will conclude . . .

- You're not really interested in the job.

- You lack good judgment.

Do

- Slow down and think about how the words you're about to say will affect the listener.

#6: Don't Say Cutesy Stuff or Use Unprofessional and Irrelevant Information in Letters and Resumes

It drives Eric Zuckerman crazy when people start their cover letters with quotes and poems. He points to a letter he got that began with several lines by Robert Frost, awkwardly and somewhat inaccurately converted to prose:

> "Two roads diverged in a wood and I took the one less traveled by, And that has made all the difference."

The writer went on to say, "My career has not been one of just circumstances, but what has been right. And that has led me to . . ." Zuckerman couldn't remember more because he didn't finish the letter.

He says that as he read it, "I wanted to know, 'What's your point? Who are you? Can we get to the meat here? I love Robert Frost, but what are you doing? You have my attention for 30 seconds. You're going to waste it while I read a poem?' The same goes when I see a resume. It's all about a glance. Make that glance count."

Another letter started: "It's that time of year we are thankful and to enjoy some quality time with friends and family." The next sentence said, "I have six years experience."

"It had nothing to do with anything," he points out.

He'd much rather get a letter that covers these three points:

1. Hello, I was excited to see that your company does such and such.

2. I noticed in your job posting you're looking for these particular experiences and skills.

3. I've been doing that exact thing and here's how I can help you.

It may "seem like a good idea to get 'cute' or super creative and try to be unique," he says. Or to "write something completely out there to get your attention or to use a crazy design. But just getting your attention is not always good," he says.

Choose Language That Accomplishes the Task

In his New York Times book review of Life Sentences, a book by William H. Gass on writing style and prose, Adam Kirsch writes: "One part of the science of rhetoric is choosing the kind of language needed for the particular task the writer wants to accomplish: sometimes fireworks are called for, sometimes a match will do." (January 20, 2012)

How do you write a rousing cover letter that enhances your chances of getting to the next step?

Think of your cover letter as an entranceway to a room. A foyer, where people get their first impression and the tone is set. You're making an entryway into the life of the employer. They're getting their first impression of you and deciding whether to go further.

Besides poetry, what doesn't work?

An e-mail that sounds like a 12-year-old wrote it. Here's a real example: "Hey! I went and check out your website and I wasn't sure if you guys had anything open. Do have any good leads for me?"

And e-mails and letters that start off badly. "Hi, how are you all?" is another true-life example.

Or starting off by telling the employer how great you are.

That is what most people do, one employer told me. "It's all about them. They go on and on about how they have this background and that degree and how they are looking for an opportunity."

"Hook me," says this employer who gets about three cover letters per week, mostly by e-mail. "Get me excited so I want to read more and feel you have something on the ball."

To write that kind of letter, you have to stop thinking "I'm supposed to write a cover letter," which will lead to a letter of stilted, uninspiring business blabber you think you're "supposed" to use. Instead, ramp up your determination to grab and hold the reader's interest. When you sit down to write, plant this in your head: *"I'm going to seize your attention and keep you reading until the very last word."*

Remember what that employer said: "Most people start off telling me how great they are." That doesn't win him over.

Instead, make that first paragraph about the *employer* and his *company*. That's what he cares about.

Yes, a great cover letter is that simple. And here's how you accomplish that. Start off with something like this: "I read about you in the XYZ report . . . " Or "Since you're looking for a resourceful and experienced manager who can oversee the daily activities of such and such, we should talk."

In the next paragraph and the one after that keep the employer in your mind. Think: What can I share to show I can improve your life and business?

Keep remembering: It's not about you. It's about them.

Don't

◻ Waste the employer's time and attention with irrelevant information in your letters and resume.

Employers will conclude . . .

◻ You don't understand their priorities.

◻ You don't know anything about them.

◻ You're not particularly efficient.

Do

◻ Think about what's on the employer's mind and immediately address it in your correspondence.

◻ Hook them in the first line and keep them reading until the end with information on how you'll help them.

#7: Don't Say "I Have Good People Skills"

There are fewer things that turn an employer's bright and hopeful eyes into bleary-eyed orbs than saying, "I'm a people person" or "I have good people skills."

You may indeed like people, get along with others, and enjoy interacting with customers and clients. Still, don't say "I'm a people person."

Why? Because everybody says "I'm a people person" or "I have good people skills" (many of whom probably have no right to those claims). The words mean nothing.

"I couldn't wait to end the conversation, which had just begun," one employer told me after interviewing an applicant. "The woman made the same mistakes I see every day. I asked her to tell me about herself. By the time she had gotten through her memorized list of strengths and that crap about being a 'people person,' I was praying my phone would ring so I could end the interview."

Why would you even say you're a "people person?" Because you think you should? It's what "they" want to hear? Or because the position you want entails dealing with others?

What job doesn't? Whether you're making sandwiches or software, preparing someone's taxes or launching an advertising campaign, you interact with others. Every day you're getting buy-in and input, enlisting help and giving feedback. No matter what your field, how large or small the company, whether you work with people, products, or ideas, whether you're 25 or 55, you need to get along with people. What employer wouldn't want that?

If this indeed is one of your greatest attributes, why not say so in a way that has some teeth and relevance to the employer? *Explain what you mean.*

Keep in mind that being "good with people" doesn't mean you're the most affable, gregarious human on planet earth. Think about what *you* do that makes you so effective. This will give you the language to explain it.

Do you speak and write in a way that makes it easy for customers, clients, and others to understand what you mean? Do you communicate often enough so they don't feel left out in the cold?

Are you effective at working through difficult issues with customers, clients, and coworkers without screaming at one another? Do you know how to get your point across and preserve the relationship at the same time? Are you pleasant, kind, respectful, and aware of other people? Do you put people at ease and quickly build trust?

These are all things that so-called "people persons" do well.

Instead of saying or writing, "I'm a people person," say something like this: "I'm very skilled in working with people. I am sensitive to others. And through my empathy and good listening skills, I can bring calm to emotional situations so we can move on to solve the problem."

When you're more specific and clear, you sound like you know yourself—and why you're valuable. And employers will like what they're hearing. They want someone who can do that. (It's covered in #12 and #16 on the list in Chapter 1.)

Or try this: "I enjoy building relationships with customers. I want to really know them and build trust, so I spend time meeting face-to-face to understand their problems."

Figure out what being a "people person" means for you so it's credible and you can expound on it.

Even better, here's the best way to show you have this valuable credential, which every employer wants: Actually *show them in how you deal with them.* Remember: *You are how you seem.* So approach prospective employers with sensitivity to their needs. Before you send an e-mail, utter a sentence, or write a word on paper, think about how it might affect them. Think through how they will view this. What do you need to say to be diplomatic? Are you being respectful of them and others you deal with in the process?

Yes, doing this and more will *show* them you are indeed a people person.

Don't

◻ Use the cliché "I'm a people person."

Employers will conclude . . .

◻ You heard it was a good thing to say.

- You don't stand out from everyone else.

- You probably don't even know what it means.

Do

- Show employers you really are effective with other people by treating them for what they are—creatures of emotions. Anticipate how your words and actions might affect them and make them feel.

- Figure out what you mean by being a "people person" and put it in words that describe your particular skills.

#8: Don't Say "That's Not an Issue"

Most job interviews have their share of squirm-provoking questions. Some questions even creep into that what-does-that-have-to-do-with-anything? zone. Other times an interviewer comes out and says or implies something that you know isn't an issue. But it is to that person or company.

It could be that:

- You've always been in nonprofit and this job is in a for-profit business.

- You're accustomed to fast-paced environments managing people and handling more responsibility, so they worry you'll be bored.

Again, it may not be an issue in *your* head. But it is for the employer. How do you respond to those concerns? You could squirm your way through it. Respond with indignant wrath. Gracefully dodge. Get defensive or brush it off in so many words or simply say, "That's not an issue."

Most people go for the latter. The problem with that is it doesn't make the concern disappear in the employer's head. You have not reassured the interviewer that it's *not* an issue simply by saying, "It's not an issue." Plus, you've missed a delicious opportunity to *show* the employer how you handle potentially sticky situations.

Not unlike the potential objections we discussed in Chapter 3, you need to address any overt or implied concerns in an artful manner.

Let's walk through an example.

Linda was interviewing for a job as a career counselor after being a teacher for 15 years. Employers were concerned that:

◻ Having been in a school setting for so long, she wouldn't understand business.

◻ She wouldn't be able to relate to adults.

◻ She would be too theoretical and not practical.

When an interviewer said, "But you don't have any experience dealing with professional adults since you've been in the educational environment your whole career," here's how Linda responded:

"I can see why that might be a concern. Perhaps it would help if I tell you a little more about my background and why I don't see that hindering me in this role."

The employer was open to that. So she went on:

"Besides teaching over the last 15 years, I developed a program helping executives be better communicators. In the summer months I worked with dozens of CEOs and managers from Fortune 500 firms and smaller companies as a consultant. I have also given workshops in healthcare, financial services, manufacturing, and government settings. So I'm very familiar with day-to-day issues people face in businesses and the various types of organizations within the work world."

Sounded pretty good, don't you think? She not only alleviated the interviewer's concern, she did it in a way that made you like her. How did she do that?

First, she acknowledged the employer's concern. Then she helped the interviewer not be concerned about it. She basically said two things:

1. I hear ya.

Most people would say, "But I *do* have experience . . . " But when you acknowledge the employer's issue, you can almost hear the sigh of relief. This helps open up the conversation.

You could also say, "Could you tell me more about your concern?" This opens the way for the employer to tell you exactly how he concluded what he did. It allows the employer to be heard.

2. Let's clear this up.

Now that you understand the issue or why the employer felt the way he did, you can correct the misunderstanding or fill in what he doesn't yet know.

Harvard professors Todd Rogers and Michael Norton point out in the *Journal of Experimental Psychology* (May 2011) that when speakers artfully dodge, listeners can fail to detect such dodges. They propose that's because the listeners' attention "is directed toward a goal of social evaluation (i.e., Do I like this person?)."

Put another way by Dale Carnegie in Rule 6 of his booklet *How to Make Our Listeners Like Us* (Dale Carnegie & Associates, Inc., 1959, 1962): "We can't win friends with a scowling face and an upbraiding voice." He adds: "Quintilian taught nineteen centuries ago that 'that which offends the ear will not easily gain admission to the mind.'"

Don't

▫ Dismiss an employer's concern by implying or saying, "That's not an issue." It will continue to bug them.

Employers will conclude . . .

▫ You're desperate.

▫ You're covering something up.

▫ You don't handle a sensitive moment well.

▫ You don't have what they need.

Do

▫ Use this as an opportunity to show the employer how well you handle sticky situations.

▫ Use this as an opportunity to show the employer how empathetic you are.

▫ Alleviate an employer's concern by acknowledging the issue and sharing concrete information on why it's not a concern.

#9: Don't Say "I Won't Do That!"

Tonya Lain of Adecco understands the importance of balancing work and life. But when you start off the interview with that—saying, in essence, that you won't or can't do something because you have "conflicts with other commitments outside of work such as school or daycare and discussing those priorities first"—it's a turnoff.

It's also a big mistake when people indicate "they aren't willing to do other tasks that aren't part of the job description," Lain says.

"When a candidate is inflexible and expects their job description to remain static, it's a big red flag for me. I've had people say they didn't like it when things changed with daily routines or that they'd prefer to have a structured schedule and to know what they would be doing specifically every day.

"Regardless of the job, employers today are looking for candidates who are self-starters, adaptable, and willing to take on responsibilities that may not come with the original job description. We look for individuals who can wear many hats and are open to getting their hands dirty to try new things and learn new skills. I tend to avoid candidates who don't demonstrate that level of flexibility." (That's #11 and #13 on the list.)

George Bradt, managing director of the executive onboarding consulting firm PrimeGenesis, eliminated one junior-level candidate based on her response to his asking her how she felt about travel.

"She started telling me where she would go and would not go." (She was also late to the interview and had an out-of-date resume.)

"I ended the interview and told her to come back when she was excited about the job, that she'd travel to Timbuktu if we wanted her to do so. I never heard back from her."

Yes, you have a life outside of work. Yes, you need to consider family obligations and other issues. But there is no need to bring them up early in your conversations with employers. You'll get to it in the appropriate way and when the time is right—preferably when the employer has said they want you for the role.

If, for example, you are asked early in the process how you feel about working after hours, you can always artfully handle such a question by saying something like this:

"I don't know exactly what the job entails yet. But I assure you that I take my work very seriously. You can feel comfortable that my personal life will not disrupt my work at the company."

That keeps the conversation going.

Unfortunately, it's very unusual for candidates to come out and say they are willing to stay at work and do what it takes to get a job done, says Lain.

But if you do say that (and mean it, of course) *you will stand out from everyone else*.

Don't

- Immediately focus on hours and talk about your limitations and expectations or your concerns about work hours or potential overtime.

Employers will conclude . . .

- You don't adapt to change well.

- You would be resistant if asked to take on different tasks.

- You're not a team player who cares about doing whatever it takes to be successful.

- You're inflexible.

- You're not eager to learn and excel.

Do

- Acknowledge your understanding that the work may not fit neatly into a 9-to-5 schedule.

- Tell the employer that you're willing to do what needs to be done to complete a project.

- Assure the employer that you're open to pitching in and helping others.

- Be open to doing what the role requires.

#10: Don't Say "I Just Want to Learn"

You'll recall I mentioned this briefly in Chapter 3, #1: Don't Act Clueless and Unprepared. It may seem like a perfectly natural response to explain why you want the job you're interviewing for when you're a recent graduate, a younger worker, or moving into an area in which you've never worked. But it doesn't fare well.

Again, it may make you sound eager—which isn't bad. But that's not enough to make an employer want to hire you. Yes, employers know you need to learn. Even seasoned folks will need to get up to speed on certain things. But you won't get hired because of that.

According to the 2011 MetLife Survey of the American Teacher: Preparing Students for College and Careers, 97 percent of executives rate strong writing skills as absolutely essential or very important and 99 percent rate problem solving as absolutely essential or very important.

Forgive me for repeating myself, but I find you can never hear this enough: Why *would* they hire you? Because you can help the company create and deliver the product it makes or service it offers. And you need to know how you will do that. Or as I left it in the last chapter: How will you justify your paycheck? So let's talk about that now.

Let's say, for example, you have a great interest in saving wetlands and trees and in safe trash disposal, and overall in making communities safe and efficient. You've targeted a career in urban planning. And now that you have your degree or new training in this area, you're looking for a job with a local or state government or an architectural or engineering firm.

The skills you've begun to develop—your potential talents—include the ability to think in terms of spatial relationships, solve problems and analyze data, and listen, communicate, and write well.

That's what it takes to be good at that work. With practice, you'll hone these skills.

Now think about your potential employer. What service does the company deliver to its customers?

Since you will have done your homework, you know that in general, the company's goal is to deliver the best input on where to put roads, houses, stores, and parks in communities. It focuses on offering the most well-thought-out solutions for too much traffic and air pollution and getting people to buses, subways, and parking lots. If you know this, when you're asked what you'd like to do at a company or how you'll contribute, you can talk about:

□ How you want to utilize these skills you've begun to develop

□ The great interest you have in doing whatever you do—such as making communities safe and efficient

□ How you'll help the company deliver its particular service to its customers

If you need help figuring out this same information for your field, go to a source like the Bureau of Labor Statistics. It's all there. This is the information age. There's no excuse for *sounding* clueless.

This is also an opportunity to show an employer that you are someone who can apply what you learn. In other words, you know how to *solve problems*—one of the most important skills you can have.

You May Not Know the Business, but Can You Solve Problems?

Problem solving is another term for mental agility, says Mike Panigel, senior vice president of human resources at Siemens. "A successful candidate knows how to quickly distill the key issues and relationships in complex situations."

A Totally Wasted Opportunity

An employer looking for an account coordinator sent a detailed, four-paragraph job description to someone who contacted him. The job hunter wrote back to the employer:

"Sounds like something I can handle for sure. I would love to learn the business."

What a waste! She had an incredible opportunity to come back with a well-thought-out rationale for why she could do the job and totally blew it.

"I laid out what we're looking for. And aside from her saying it sounds like something she could handle and would love to learn, I don't know how she would satisfy what I'm looking for," says the employer.

"I'm glad she'd love to learn the business, but why would I want to teach it to her? She didn't give me any reason to meet her. She didn't demonstrate passion for what we do. No initiative to find out. She showed lackluster communication skills through her one-sentence quips from her BlackBerry instead of writing something sincere and persuasive that would make me overlook that she had no experience or background related to what we do.

"It would be a big leap of faith on my part to bring someone so inexperienced onboard and invest my time and resources in their development. She gave me nothing that would make me want to take the leap. She hadn't looked at our website or Facebook page or investigated us or our industry to see if she'd truly want to be part of it. She didn't counter my concern that she may be looking for a job and not a career in our field. She may think this could be right up her alley, but she didn't show me that she's right up our alley."

Don't

▫ Solely focus on your need and desire to learn.

Employers will conclude . . .

▫ You're only there to learn and then will leave.

▫ You don't understand anything about the business.

Do

▫ Conduct your homework. Know a company's goals and explain how you'll use your skills to help it meet them.

▫ Emphasize your passion for the industry and its mission.

▫ Show your eagerness to learn, excel, and solve problems.

▫ Understand how you'll justify a paycheck.

▫ Give examples of how you have applied problem solving skills to understand key issues and relationships.

#11: Don't Say Anything That's Gobbledygook

I don't understand half the things job hunters say. And neither do would-be employers.

I'll ask people the type of culture they want to work in and they'll say or write, "ROWE." (I since learned it means Results-Only Work Environment.)

I'll ask them to tell me about their expertise and they'll say that they know all about "gift proposals," or "build and grow programs," "random walk," or "pack out labs." Or someone will describe himself as a "person-centered change agent who drives results through actionable learning frameworks."

When someone rattles off these terms and phrases that are perfectly understandable to them but Greek to me, I get distracted. I am preoccupied, trying to figure out what they could possibly mean.

Based on my unscientific poll of highly intelligent professionals representing a broad range of occupations—and who hire—I'm not alone.

People check out when they don't understand what you're saying. They go off into never-never land trying to make sense of your words within the context of their world. They're *not listening* to you anymore.

For example, when I asked people what goes through their heads when they hear or see this word—ROWE—here's what they said: One person thought of the name of the founders of a bank he had as clients. Someone else thought it meant Rest of World.

The phrase "random walk" (which is a mathematical formulation used in such fields as computer science, economics, and physics) brought to writer Linda Vaccariello's mind, "What I do on Mondays when I have writer's block and need to get away from the computer."

She envisioned a "gift proposal" (a way to make a charitable donation) as "what my husband and I do instead of giving one another presents. We say to each other, 'Should we buy ourselves a new dishwasher for Christmas this year?'"

Gobbledygook distracts interviewers. When you use vague, imprecise, and stale language, you're not helping them get to know you. In some cases, it annoys them.

"It tends to make you sound smug and deliberately inconsiderate," says Vaccariello. "Or, if the language is highly technical, nerdy. And there's something sort of adolescent about it. As if you're still trying to use the 'special words' that mom and dad don't know."

If you're trying to make a career change or are in the midst of a job hunt in a different industry, such talk can have a similar effect in conversations with potential employers. You will not get through to them.

According to the International Listening Association (yes, there are people who do listen), the most frequently reported listening barriers include lack of interest in the speaker's subject and thinking of another topic or "detouring" because of what the speaker has said.

So watch out for language that is lazy, imprecise mumbo jumbo and jargon that someone outside (maybe even inside) your industry wouldn't get.

These are "phrases tacked together like the sections of a pre-fabricated hen-house," said author and critic George Orwell in his 1946 essay "Politics and the English Language," which still has relevance today.

Be on constant guard and make a conscious effort not to surrender to "sheer cloudy vagueness," said Orwell. This applies to writing, such as your resume or cover letters, as well as to speaking. When you sit down to write, ask yourself, What do I want to say? How can I best say that? What example illustrates my point? Can this be said in a shorter way? Will this make a lick of sense to anyone but me and my colleagues?

OTHER WAYS YOU MISS OUT WITH GOBBLEDYGOOK

In Chapter 3 I mentioned not being overly formal or too casual. This seems like another good time to bring that up in more detail. Specifically, this type of talk includes:

▫ Meaningless one- and two-word responses such as "Awesome!" "Wow!" "No worries." "No problem."

If you are truly awed, explain what awes you. This is your chance to show how passionate you feel about the work or the mission of the company (#14 on the list).

When an employer describes what the job entails and you simply say, "No problem," you've missed a *huge* opportunity. Here's where you can go into detail about the time you did something just like that and how you made a difference.

□ Sounding like a public radio underwriting message.

I support public broadcasting, but be wary of sounding like one of those underwriting messages that forbid qualitative claims and first- or second-person pronouns. They also tend to use passive, rather than active language. In other words, don't say these kinds of things: "I endeavor to" or "We strive to endeavor . . . " It's not how people talk. And no one will know what you're talking about.

The same goes for your cover letters. Stay away from writing stilted sentences such as, "I would be very enthused with the opportunity to interview for this new position." Who says that?

Don't

□ Use terms, phrases, and acronyms that might not be clear to others.

□ Use imprecise language and mumbo jumbo.

Employers will conclude . . .

□ You're not an effective communicator.

□ You don't "get it."

□ You lack empathy.

Do

□ Take advantage of the opportunity to share clear, concise details that illustrate your contributions and your enthusiasm.

▫ Figure out what you want to say and find the simplest way to say it.

#12: Don't Use Non-Words, Fillers, and Other Annoying Things

Although it's nearly impossible to say for sure, there are at least 250,000 distinct English words, according to the Oxford University Press, which publishes the *Oxford English Dictionary*. Some linguists say there are over one million words and that the number is growing.

Even so, be wary of using *non-words*. These are words that are either misspelled, mispronounced, or are combinations or incorrect derivations of real words. A few examples include "flustrated," "supposebly," "orientated," "irregardless" and such words as this from the Oxford University Press vault of non-words: "glocalization."

Non-words also include vocal fillers. These are "Um," "uh," "ya know," and the one that makes me crazy: "like" or "I'm like."

They "can destroy your presentation, annoy people, hurt your credibility, and make listeners tense," says Kurt W. Mortensen, author of *The Laws of Charisma* (AMACOM, 2011).

Such non-words are worse than sloppy, says Ben Decker, president of Decker Communications. "They are lazy and distracting."

Often used because people don't want silence, he says, they "let comfort be their guide when it comes to communications," heading straight for the "ums," "uhs," and "likes."

This one comes from the Small But Really Annoying Things department. But since this small thing can have ramifications in your job search, it's worth a mention, right?

That was it. The small, really annoying thing. Did you catch it? The usage of "Right?" with that question mark at the end. It's how many people talk, ending about every fifth sentence with "Right?" or a combination: "You know what I mean, right?"

But they don't listen for or really want a response.

It's not new, but more pervasive. Here's what happens as result. Let's say someone is describing a project they worked on. They say: "Everyone on the team is expected to speak up if there is a problem, right?"

Saying that prompts you to think, "How would I know?" which leads you to wonder if this person was sure about what he was saying. Or you wonder, "Are you asking me if I agree that everyone on the team is expected to speak up?"

When I asked an executive who uses "Right?" at the end of her sentences if she even knew she did it, she said, "Yes, on occasion." She adds that she hears it from others, then ends up saying it herself.

"When I hear it from other people it drives me crazy," she says. "I feel irritated with the individual. I want to say, 'get on with your point and quit throwing out extraneous blah blah blah and asking for my approval.'"

Why do people do it? Maybe, she suggests, it's because we don't want to offend anyone. As a result, though, "The person is irritating, which is another type of offensiveness."

An employer who had been interviewing a lot told me he too finds it irritating. "It's a subconscious device to get someone to agree with you whether you do or not."

Another employer says, "It represents insecurity. It's as if the person needs constant validation that they're right."

Employers have a similar feeling when someone's sentences rise at the end of every statement. It's as if the person can't make a declarative statement about anything.

When you end your sentences in a question or with "Right?" the impression is that you're hedging. It sounds as if you're not sure you're committed to what you're saying. Or you're trying to get me to agree.

This is called a "tag question," according to Dr. David Silva, professor of linguistics at the University of Texas at Arlington, whom I once interviewed for my column.

Silva agrees that in using tag questions, "there's something to the idea of fostering a certain type of relationship between the speaker and the hearer, one that seeks to build mutual understanding and shared attitudes."

Wherever it comes from, it comes down to this: You sound as if you're speaking without the courage of your convictions. It's irritating to the person you're trying to have a conversation with. And that's no small thing. Right?

If any of these speech patterns are a problem for you (and even if you don't think they are), record yourself. Ask others to count how many repetitive, irritating non-words you say per minute. Or how many times you say "Right?" at the end of a point, or end everything with a question.

But most of all, replace non-words such as "I'm like" with pauses. Decker advises that as you're about to say, "And I'm like," you should just stop.

And while we're on the topic of words, fluency with the written word is just as imperative and something else employers are looking at intently.

When it comes to writing, "Being able to get your point across means the difference between success and failure," says Mike Panigel of Siemans.

And BAE Systems may ask for a writing sample to "literally see if the candidate can write," says Curt Gray, senior vice president, human resources and administration.

Writing Well Is a Requirement at UPS

At UPS, workers must be able to communicate clear and concise messages to "investigate, analyze, and report their findings in a professional manner," says Matt Lavery, managing director of corporate talent acquisition. So they are watching for indications of it in everything you write.

If you want to move up in your career, writing is key. The higher up you go, the more writing you'll do—everything from performance reviews to proposals and persuasive arguments. Most important, your writing is a reflection of what's going on your head. If you can't write well, employers are going to conclude you can't think clearly either (#2 on their list.)

Don't

□ Say "And I'm like . . . "

□ Make up words.

□ End your sentences going up or asking, "Right?" or "You know what I mean, right?"

□ Talk superfast.

Employers will conclude . . .

□ You're lazy.

□ You're immature.

□ You won't present yourself well in front of clients and customers.

- You don't know the difference between hanging out with your friends and acting like a professional.

- You are insecure or need constant validation.

- You aren't sure about what you're saying or don't believe it.

Do

- Ask others for feedback on how you come across.

- Record yourself to count how often you say non-words such as "like" and "I'm like" and "um," "uh," and "ya know."

- Take a critical look at how you write and whether you communicate clearly and concisely.

#13: Don't Use Buzzwords

I remember when the word "innovative" started popping up on everyone's resume and then on LinkedIn profiles. So many people pasted it into their list of laudable virtues that in 2010, LinkedIn's chief data scientist calculated it was the second most overused buzzword in its U.S. members' profiles. In response to that discovery, resume writers warned: Get "innovative" off your resume and LinkedIn profile!

I say, not so fast. I dislike buzzwords immensely. But before you start chopping, let's look at what you're trying to say and how to replace it with better language.

The problem with what used to be perfectly fine words like "innovative" as well as "results-oriented" and "problem solver"—two others from LinkedIn's list of overused buzzwords—is that their overuse (as is the case with "I'm a people person") makes them meaningless. You end up sounding like everyone else.

The catch is to truly understand the essence of your particular innovative ways. Because being innovative—which results in new, better, more effective products and processes—is clearly what every business needs. And if you can help a business see that you are such a being, the employer will surely want to chat.

So what does it mean to be someone who brings innovation to their work? And are you that person?

I like the way writer Janet Rae-Dupree described it in a *New York Times* article (February 3, 2008). "Innovation is a slow process of accretion, building small insight upon interesting fact upon tried-and-true process."

Innovation, or that "aha" moment, grows "out of hours of thought and study," said Jim Marggraff, inventor of the LeapFrog Fly pentop computer and creator of the LeapPad Learning System, in Rae-Dupree's article. This is "followed by a ton of work" and "a huge amount of determination and effort to follow through," says Marggraff.

Look at the phrases he uses to describe innovation: *Hours of thought and study . . . followed by a ton of work. A huge amount of determination and effort to follow through.*

Does that describe you? Do you have those qualities? If so, have your efforts led to better, more effective products or processes? If so, say so.

Don't just say "I'm innovative" in your cover letter or conversation. Say:

"I'm willing to put thought and study into figuring out a solution to a given problem."

Then give an example of how you did that:

"For example, in my last job as an administrative assistant to the president, I spent months researching and then developing a system that tracked sales information and cut days of work down to minutes."

Or: "I devoted hours of thought to how to better connect with our company's target market and devised a program that doubled sales."

In most cases, it's best to scrap other overused terms including "change agent" who "drives results" or "delivers actionable results." Instead figure out what this means, use meaningful words to describe it, and give an example of how you do that.

In the 2009 Society for Human Resource Management (SHRM) poll, employers suggested that candidates not use the following phrases—and I concur:

- This is my dream job.

- I think outside the box.

- I'm results-oriented.

- I'm a team player.

- I'm a people person.

- I take initiative.

Don't

- Fill up your resume and cover letters with buzzwords that have been said a thousand times thinking that they "sound good."

Employers will conclude . . .

- You're using words you think employers want to hear but you can't back up.

- You can't write or communicate very well.

▫ You read a lot of business books but don't really know what you mean when you repeat the words.

Do

▫ Think through how you are truly innovative, a "change agent," and how you do "drive results," and what that means. Write meaningful examples that illustrate these qualities and show you understand how those phrases relate to the work a company does.

#14: Don't Say "Goo Moring"

Yes, "goo moring" is exactly how someone began an e-mail to an employer. And this person didn't get the time of day.

Employers don't mess around with careless communications, misspellings, and typographical errors. Of the 500 hiring managers SHRM polled, 58 percent said typos or grammatical errors in a cover letter and/or resume "were a major problem/deal breaker." Forty-one percent said they were somewhat of a problem. That only leaves 1 percent who said, Typo? No problemo.

There's just something about a typo or other error staring up at you from the page. There's no denying it. And to an employer it says "sloppy worker."

"Misspellings in letters and resumes show lack of caring, professionalism, as well as [a lack of] pride in themselves and their work," says Dianne Durkin, president of Loyalty Factor.

"If a person's resume has spelling errors, they will not even have the opportunity for a phone interview," says Rob Basso. "It's a reflection of your skills and work ethic and it should be flawless."

"I get tons of letters and resumes with spelling errors," says Eric Zuckerman. "When you have so many applicants, you have to come up with your own system to go through them. A spelling error makes me pass on them. They could have all the experience in the world, but presentation can make a difference."

Remember Bill Strauss, chairman of the law firm Strauss & Troy (Chapter 2)? When he was trying to make his way though a batch of resumes and letters for the firm's part-time marketing director job, he started looking at the resume and application itself as a marketing piece, "as if this is an example of their work."

He says he "looked for typos, grammar, writing, and persuasion skills of the person who was in the act of marketing to me." From there he eliminated applicants right and left.

The person who got an interview, and who the company eventually hired, "looked like a person who cared about the appearance of her work product"—an important value to this employer.

Don't

- Let typographical errors and misspellings end up in any document you create.

Employers will conclude . . .

- You don't care about your work that much.

- You don't pay attention to details.

- You'll be sloppy in your work.

Do

- Read, reread, read again, and then show everything you write to another set of eyes before you send it to an employer.

#15: Don't Say You Know Me (When You Don't) or Tell Other Lies

It seems a week doesn't go by without getting a LinkedIn message from a stranger who wants to "connect," saying, for example, "We worked together in Quebec at the such-and-such dog food company."

Do you think my memory is that foggy that I don't remember ever living in Quebec working at a dog food company?

I can't be any more clear than this: Don't contact potential employers through LinkedIn—the chief online network used for business and job hunting—or other social media and lie about your relationship.

For that matter, don't lie about *any* information you post anywhere on your profile, in your resume, or when you talk about yourself.

I'm all for being strategic about what you say and using relevant information that positions you the way you want to be seen. But that's where I draw the line. There is a difference between persuasive marketing and being deceitful.

While we're on the subject, how *do* you connect with other professionals on LinkedIn in an honest, straightforward way? The first "do" actually is a "don't": If you want to get in touch with someone you don't know, do not send a request to "Join my network on LinkedIn." That's like saying, "You don't know me. So you can't really trust me. But I'd still like you to hand over your list of contacts so they can help me and my career."

The best approach is to ask for an introduction to that person you don't know—let's call her Milly—through someone else who does know Milly. Or, send Milly an InMail, a LinkedIn feature that shoots a direct message to Milly. But like any other correspondence, *personalize* your note. Tell Milly what you admire about her and her work or how you've been following her since you first heard her speak at that dog food conference in Boston.

Again, I'll repeat: You should never, ever send one of those generic "I'd like to add you to my network" messages to someone. Unless it's someone you know well and see regularly.

Have no doubt, if you lie, you will be found out. People in your network will out you.

"People have gotten comfortable with social networking where they're always putting their best face on. It's all about good news and almost trying to one-up the next person," points out Krista Canfield, manager of corporate communications at LinkedIn.

But a professional network is different. "You shouldn't take liberties and say things that aren't true," she says. Don't, for example, create your profile in German. It makes people think you speak German, when you don't.

When it comes to your resume, your letters, your online profiles. or your own website, don't:

- Misrepresent the number of years you've worked at a job.

- Exaggerate your accomplishments and skills or take credit for something you didn't do.

- Misrepresent the size of a company you worked for.

- Claim to have educational credentials or degrees from institutions you didn't earn.

- Inflate titles.

- Claim to speak a foreign language fluently when you only took a few years of classes in high school.

Saying untruths is the kiss of death in a job hunt. Not to mention that if you do get hired and found out later, the consequences will be dire.

You've undoubtedly heard of some higher-profile professionals who cooked up educational credentials and then, after being found out, got kicked off boards or suspended, or they resigned: David Edmondson, chief executive of RadioShack, resigned after lying about having a college degree. Motivational speaker Denis Waitley was forced off the board of USANA Health Sciences after it was discovered he hadn't received a degree he had claimed. Yahoo CEO Scott Thompson was accused of listing a bogus degree on his resume and subsequently stepped down.

Some people who fudge credentials think they have good reason. Take the frantic person who wrote me a few years back begging for advice. He explained that he had been working as a contract worker for a company then became an employee. During the hiring process, he submitted his resume and application.

"I lied about my education," he wrote. He had just learned that the company was conducting a background check and is "very nervous about what to do if they found out I lied. I know it was wrong. I thought if I put that I graduated with a degree that I would qualify for a higher salary. I was scared they may not hire me. It was out of desperation that I embellished my education."

I once heard a professor from Brandeis University on NPR's *Talk of the Nation* say that most lying is pragmatic. The more situational pressure someone is under, the more apt that person is to lie, he said. Sometimes people believe that everybody else is cheating. In the case of resumes, you may think that everybody else is inflating their background. So to be competitive you have to do it as well.

Most people take integrity seriously. When you stretch the truth or out-and-out lie, it makes someone wonder what else you're not being up front about.

Don't

▫ Contact employers or others via LinkedIn and say "You know me" when you don't, or indicate that "You are a Friend" when you're not.

▫ Concoct stories, stretch the truth, or fib about your credentials or mislead employers about your background.

Employers will conclude . . .

▫ You'll be dishonest about other things.

▫ You lack integrity.

▫ There's a whiff of "something not right" about you.

Do

▫ Create persuasive, strategic marketing documents that support your objective and position you the way you want to be seen, and that are 100 percent on the level.

▫ Use professional networks like LinkedIn strategically. Ask for introductions to people you don't know through people you do know. Or send personalized messages through the InMail feature.

five

□ □ □ □ □ □ □ □ □ □

10 Things You Should Never Wear

I have gotten over the shock of seeing someone out and about in their pajamas at, say, Bob Evans or Target. Just woke up and forgot to change before you left the house? I suppose it's possible. And no one seems to care.

But a job interview? Believe me, employers care what you piece together and slip onto your body when you meet for a face-to-face chat.

In fact, they are appalled at what some people show up wearing. Most employers have at least one "I can't believe he [or she] wore that!" story.

Appalling outfits include leather vest with no shirt; swimsuit and cover-up; leather pants and cowboy boots; Bermuda shorts; jogging suit; and yes, even pajamas with slippers, according to the staffing service OfficeTeam.

Whether you're going to an interview at a bank or a retail establishment, what you wear and how you are groomed *matter*. A lot. It's the first thing people see when you meet. They will size you up based on how you look. And your clothes say a lot about your judgment and level of professionalism—two extremely important criteria.

Yes, *how* dressed up and *how* conservative you get depend on the job, the industry, and the company. But some things are just *never* appropriate. We'll talk about that next.

Consider This When Looking Through Your Closet

There are two factors to mull over when you're standing in front of your closet to decide what to wear (which by the way, you should do days in advance of the interview—just in case something needs cleaning or mending).

1. THE JOB AND THE INDUSTRY

Ask yourself: How do people in this industry dress? Law and accounting firms and banks are some of the most conservative businesses. Even if you're not a lawyer or banker but are applying to work in a law firm or bank, consider the environment. It's a place where you need to engender trust in your clientele. You're dealing with very important issues. You want to be taken seriously. You'll be expected to dress more conservatively in these industries.

If you're interviewing at a retail establishment, an advertising agency, or a design or architectural firm, you can be less conservative. But you still need to dress like a professional. And of course, it depends on the job. In some industries, if you showed up in a suit you'd never get the job. (More on that in a minute.)

Also ask yourself: How do people in *this* job dress? Account executives in an ad agency will be more buttoned-down than a copywriter. But copywriters still meet with clients. Office managers and receptionists deal with the public as well as with customers or clients, and can be the first person someone sees.

So dress for the job *and* the industry.

2. THE IMPRESSION YOU WANT TO MAKE

What do you want people to think when they see you? For sure, you want to be seen as a professional with good judgment. Other impressions might include these: Highly successful. Detail-oriented. Discreet. Trustworthy. Stylish and tasteful.

In most cases, when in doubt, dress up, rather than down. And as Eric Zuckerman, president of PacTeam Group, says, "Regardless of the company's culture, do not show up dressed casually. Even if a company's dress code allows shorts and T-shirts, you do not work there, so that dress code does not apply to you."

Regardless of your industry or job, the following 10 things will detract from your being seen as a professional with good judgment. Don't do them. Since employers' conclusions about these ten "Don'ts" were all very similar, I've listed the "Employers Will Conclude" section near the end of this chapter.

#1: Don't Wear Plaid, Hawaiian, or Animal Print Shirts or T-Shirts with or Without Wording

Greg Gottsacker, principal of North Star Business Systems in Minneapolis, says he has seen "a lot of folks who didn't know how to dress for an interview."

Most of the tech types he's interviewed think a clean Hawaiian shirt and jeans are OK. But, he admits, he's old school. He'd like to see a dark suit and tie. There's nothing wrong with that—especially for a management position.

A vice president who works in information technology for a large company in the Midwest says she expects "conservative business attire." If you're interviewing for a management or leadership position, she expects a suit. For "individual contributors" a conservative look—but not a suit—is expected.

Minimally, for a man, dark slacks and a jacket with a plain long-sleeved white or light blue shirt works well. It depends on the region, the company, and the position. This applies to most traditional businesses.

On the other hand, Alex Churchill of VonChurch, the recruiting firm that hires workers for the digital entertainment industry, sees things a bit differently. He says, "You wouldn't get the job if you wear a suit. We do not conform to the usual 9 to 5. We have a different set of rules."

So if an applicant came to an interview at VonChurch wearing a suit, it would be clear to him that the person "does not understand our industry or values." It's an industry, as he puts it, that does "not work harder if we have a piece of cloth called a tie around our necks. We are valued on our work and results and not by our wardrobe." But you still don't want to show up looking like a bum.

In this "no-suits" industry, Churchill suggests men and women wear clothes that are "smart yet casual. Jeans. Smart shirt. Smart shoes."

If in doubt, he suggests you call a recruiter in advance and ask what the dress code would be.

In more traditional industries, a dark solid or subtly patterned suit (wool or wool blend) is still appropriate for most interviews. T-shirts (with or without words or pictures) and plaid shirts are not a good idea for any interview.

In Rochester, New York, where Karen D'Angelo is a human

resources associate at the marketing firm Catalyst, a more buttoned-down look is preferred. When the company interviewed candidates for a client services position, she was looking for a candidate who could handle a retail banking client and "interface with C-suite–level bank executives. So we expected a high level of professionalism," she says.

One candidate, for whom she had high hopes, had a resume that reflected professionalism, but his presence did not. When he showed up at the interview, "He wore a plaid shirt and khaki pants. No tie. No folder with resumes to share. He carried no notebook to capture any notes. No portfolio. The most basic of basics, and he failed the test."

What did she conclude? "He didn't care enough about the position to dress for success."

Don't wear

- Sweatshirts, T-shirts, or shirts with Hawaiian or other loud prints.

- Casual khaki pants.

Do wear

- Cotton or synthetic long-sleeved, white or light blue shirts.

- Wool or wool blend suit jacket and pants.

- Dark slacks.

#2: Don't Wear Nose and Tongue Rings

A recruiter in Pittsburgh describes a young woman who "looked great when I interviewed her." So the recruiter sent her to meet with the president of a bank. Unfortunately, the woman showed up for the interview with nose and tongue rings (along with her mini-skirt and low-cut top, which we'll talk about next).

People at the bank—the recruiter's client—rushed the young woman out of the interview. The president "was shocked that anyone would show up in that outfit just going into a bank, let alone going there to interview," she says. "I had to apologize all over the place. I am glad I didn't lose the account."

Some people say, "Well, that's just who I am and if someone doesn't like it, too bad." Yes, you're certainly free to express your individuality. But there's a good chance a lot of employers won't like it. And that's their prerogative, too.

Don't wear

□ Nose and tongue rings and other facial piercings.

Do

□ Remove facial piercing.

#3: Don't Wear Revealing Blouses or Strapless, Cropped Tops

Yes, people wear those things to interviews—a lot. A particular candidate came dressed in a low-cut, revealing blouse with a super-short skirt, says real estate specialist Chantay Bridges of Clear-Choice Realty & Associates in Beverly Hills. She didn't have a chance.

"The managers didn't consider this candidate a serious contender for the position," she says. Some of them said, "Did she think she was interviewing for Hooters?"

What did they conclude about her? She lacks wisdom, does not exercise discretion, and has poor judgment. And, "If an employer has to tell you to dress professionally for an interview, what else will have to be communicated to you that's common knowledge to everyone else?" she says.

When deciding on your interview outfit, keep this in mind: Most of the clothes that women wear in work situations portrayed on television programs are not acceptable. It's television, not the real world.

Stick with blouses that are buttoned up and tops that do not reveal cleavage, your back, your stomach, or your underwear. And on top of that, wear a solid-color jacket.

Don't wear

- Provocative clothing.

- Tank tops, low-cut blouses, and strapless or halter tops.

- Anything that reveals cleavage, your back, your stomach, or your underwear.

Do wear

- Tailored blouses or simple knits that coordinate with your jacket.

❝Appearance can't be ignored for any level position. But certainly higher-level executives really need to project a professional image. Men tend to be the worst performers—unshaven, flip-flops, old clothes. Women—too much makeup, strong perfume, plunging necklines, expensive clothes that fit four sizes ago. Candidates should scope out the environment before an interview. You can't be overdressed; you can be underdressed.❞
—Charley Polachi, partner at executive search firm Polachi

#4: Don't Wear Super-Short Skirts or Miniskirts

Miniskirts may go in and out of style over the years. But they have never been the right thing to wear to a job interview.

When Dallas-based writer Sami Swan Thompson worked for a small, conservative law firm, a young woman showed up to interview for a receptionist position in a tube top, miniskirt, flip-flop sandals, and a suit jacket.

"I suppose she thought that the suit jacket compensated for the rest," Thompson says.

She says she doesn't usually judge by appearances, "But come on! It was a job interview at a law firm. I concluded that the woman was either an idiot or had suffered some kind of brain injury in her closet that caused her to select such inappropriate clothing for an interview. Unless her house was on fire, and those were the only clothes she could reach as she jumped off her balcony."

What's the right skirt length? Keep in mind that when you sit, your skirt creeps up three inches. So pick a skirt that stops at your knees. And watch out for skirts with slits—even if they're longer—since your skirt will open to where that slit opens.

Don't wear

- Skorts, sundresses, or miniskirts.

- Clothes that show your thighs.

- Jackets with big, bold prints.

Do wear

- A suit with pants or a skirt that stops at your knees, or a skirt or tailored pants (that are not skintight) and a solid-color jacket.

□ A tailored dress and a jacket.

□ Well-coordinated outfits.

#5: Don't Wear Beachwear Such as Flip-Flops, Sandals, Sneakers, or Rubber-Soled Deck Shoes

The worst part of the outfit the candidate wore to an interview at a pharmaceutical firm were the thongs, says recruiter Abby Kohut of Springfield, New Jersey. "The same kind I wear to the beach!"

"Many people in human resources do not like seeing open-toed shoes—which personally doesn't bother me. But thongs are completely inappropriate," she says.

What did she conclude about that person? For one, the candidate had poor judgment. "Why someone would decide to wear thongs on an interview is beyond me. The lack of suit was bad enough."

Second, "It made me believe she didn't want to impress us, so she probably wasn't all that interested in the job." The candidate did not make it to round two.

Don't wear

□ Flip-flops, sandals, slippers, or athletic shoes.

Do wear

□ Closed-toe conservative leather or man-made shoes.

#6: Don't Wear Jeans, Stretch Pants, Leggings, or Shorts

How you present yourself to Ginny Baldridge, an executive image consultant in St. Louis, matters. Yet, when she interviewed a man in his 50s for a public relations job, he seemed unconcerned." He appeared for the interview wearing jeans, an extremely wrinkled golf shirt, and rubber-soled brown deck shoes with white socks," she says.

"I was completely taken aback that the woman who submitted a wonderfully professional and polished resume would come to an interview dressed like she was going to clean out her basement," says Dianne Daniels, small-business owner.

He was also carrying "a cheap, nylon briefcase" and had a spiral-bound notebook—"the type a third-grader would carry."

She was so shocked by his appearance that "at first I could not get past my initial feelings. This gentleman knew I was an executive image consultant, yet he had made no effort to dress in a way that would make me even want to carry on an interview."

She concluded, "He was lazy, did not pay any attention to detail, and was too cheap to buy a decent notebook or briefcase. He was also someone I would never trust with my business. How could he represent me or my company?"

When Dianne Daniels worked for a government entity in the Northeast (today she has her own image consulting and coaching firm in Norwich, Connecticut), she once interviewed a woman who came dressed in zebra print stretch pants and a pink cutoff T-shirt "with a questionable message on the front."

Her first thought: She had walked into the wrong office. "I was completely taken aback that the woman who submitted a wonderfully professional and polished resume would come to an interview dressed like she was going to clean out her basement," says Daniels.

How did this woman's appearance affect her? "There was nothing about the outfit that was professional or would engender trust. It made her look sloppy, lackadaisical, and completely inappropriate for a business office. Her appearance made her look as if she did not understand the basic rules of dressing for the job" and put into question other skills.

She was a strong candidate, says Daniels. But "the visual impression was too hard to get past" and she didn't hire the woman.

Don't wear

- Jeans, spandex, leggings, shorts, exercise pants, or capris.

- White socks.

- Anything that could pass for wardrobe from a John Waters movie.

Do wear

- Dark socks that go up to the middle of your calf.

- Conservative slacks, shirts, blouses, and jackets.

#7: Don't Wear High, High Heels or Patterned Hose

I like shoes as much as the next gal. But six-and-a-half-inch towering heels, two-and-a-half-inch platforms that infer rock-star status, and lavishly decorated heels with embroidery and light-catching crystals? Not for interviews.

April Lewis worked for a nonprofit organization that had openings for business development and public relations positions. She says candidates came to interviews "in patterned pantyhose and heels so high they could hardly walk."

As a result, "we concluded that the individuals were not professional, were uneducated, and had no common sense. If you can't dress for a job interview, how can you represent an organization?" None of them were hired.

As for whether to wear hose at all, well, no one totally agrees.

Most etiquette experts say yes, women should wear hose to interviews. Others—myself included—feel that hose (at least in warm climates and in the summer) make you seem outdated.

It seems "totally acceptable not to wear hose to an interview," says Chantay Bridges. By wearing them you can be "perceived as old-fashioned or looking like a senior." But she agrees with most others—it depends on where you're interviewing. Since you're trying to blend in with the corporate culture, consider wearing hose if it's an "ultra-super-conservative company and all their senior staff wear them," she says. But if it's a place "with more of a lax, hip, fun atmosphere," skip them.

If you do wear hose, don't wear the ones with patterns and wild colors.

Don't wear

- Fishnet or patterned hose.

- Bare legs in conservative environments.

- Stilettos or open-toed shoes.

Do wear

- Conservative leather or fabric shoes you can walk in.

- Polished, closed-toe pumps with heels that aren't worn out.

#8: Don't Wear Unflattering, Ill-Fitting Clothing That Needs Cleaning

Until you pull your clothes out of the closet and assemble them on your body for a complete outfit, you never know how they fit and if anything needs mending or cleaning.

One employer described a candidate who wore an outfit with

buttons and pockets that were gaping. The top seam along the shoulder of her blouse looked like it was pinching off the circulation in her arms. It all made the woman, who was interviewing for a job at a private school, seem well . . . unaware.

The employer says the first thing she concluded was the candidate "was doing the best she could with what she had, and I had compassion. I also knew that she was a new mom and was still carrying the baby fat, and that she was poor, and I had been in that position myself in the past. But there was also an underlying concern that she didn't see or care that her clothes were very ill-fitting, and that that lack of self-awareness would transfer to her job performance."

Employers will understand that you may not have a lot of money to put into clothing. You don't have to buy expensive clothes. But do wear an outfit that fits and is clean.

Don't wear

◻ Frayed edges or anything torn.

◻ Pins instead of buttons.

◻ Clothes that are too big or snug.

Do wear

◻ Well-fitting clothes that have been dry-cleaned.

#9: Don't Wear Overkill Jewelry, Makeup, and Other Accessories

What may be great for a party doesn't fit at work. So no huge earrings or clanging bracelets.

The same goes for other accessories such as hats and giant scarves. And make sure you remove any electronic doodads that are hanging on your body. Remember the man who walked into an interview wearing iPod earphones that I mentioned in Chapter 3? As Kevin Sheridan, senior vice president of HR Optimization at Avatar HR Solutions said, it was "not a great first impression during the handshake."

Watch out for too much makeup, perfume, or cologne, and also for smelling like smoke. And stay away from two-inch long, neon-colored nails that look like weapons.

Don't wear

▫ Sunglasses—on your face or on top of your head.

▫ Headphones around your neck or in your ears.

▫ Long fingernails with bright or specialty polish.

▫ Green, purple, or other unnatural hair color.

Do wear

▫ A tasteful amount of makeup.

▫ Limited amounts of tasteful jewelry.

#10: Don't Wear Uniforms

It seems obvious, but some people actually show up in uniforms emblazoned with the name of their former employer. Don't.

Do wear

▫ A suit or nice slacks, shirt, and a jacket or skirt.

Don't wear

▫ Clothes with wording on them.

▫ Name tags and uniforms from other companies.

Follow these ten rules or employers will conclude:

- *You don't care that much about the position.*

- *You don't have the level of professionalism the job requires.*

- *You don't fit the company's culture.*

- *You don't understand the fundamentals of running a professional business.*

- *You're lazy.*

- *You don't pay attention to detail.*

- *You have poor judgment.*

- *You can't be trusted with their business.*

- *If you don't know how to dress professionally, you won't know other things that are common knowledge to everyone else.*

- *You're immature and irresponsible.*

- *You don't have leadership presence.*

- *Your appearance is a distraction.*

- *You lack common sense.*

" *While I don't expect someone to wear a three-piece suit, I expect someone to come dressed appropriately, in business formal wear. The expectation is dress to impress. There's no reason you can't let your personality show through in some of your accessory choices. But demonstrate to me that you are a professional and I should treat you as such."*

—Rob Basso, owner of Advantage Payroll Services

Details, Details

Everything from head to toe matters. Your nails, your hair, how you smell. Susan Jacobsen, president of LUV2XLPR, a public relations firm in Alexandria, Virginia, can't forget a man who arrived at the interview "sweating profusely and smelling terribly."

Apparently, it was a very hot, humid day, and "instead of taking a cab he decided to walk the ten blocks and arrived overheated, disheveled, and out of breath," says Jacobsen. In the first seconds of meeting him she was affected negatively. And that's how she remembers him.

A Midwestern information technology executive says a man she interviewed for a director position over the phone sounded good. But when he appeared for a face-to-face interview, "I was immediately put off by his appearance. He had long, dirty fingernails, very unkempt hair, and a shirt and suit that needed a good trip to the dry cleaner."

She concluded that he "didn't have the leadership presence needed for the position and his appearance was a distraction. Unfortunately for him, because of his appearance the interview was over before it started."

On the other hand, one job hunter I know was thinking about how to make sure he looked the part for a bank management job. The position was for an institution in Venezuela, and his interview was in Florida. He had just gotten out of the Peace Corps. He bought a nice suit. He spoke fluent Spanish. But, he thought, "Maybe I should have a briefcase to look more like a banker." So he bought a briefcase and carried it in. He got the job.

When polled by the Society for Human Resource Management, 95 percent of employers said dressing both too casually and too provocatively was somewhat of a problem or a deal breaker.

Before you walk out the door

- Make sure you're not missing any buttons.

- Remove all tags from new clothing.

- Make sure you're free from lint and pet fur.

Don't carry . . .

- A cheap-looking nylon briefcase.

- A big, bulky briefcase. (You don't need to carry that much stuff to an interview.)

- A humongous purse.

- Book bags and backpacks.

Do bring . . .

- A portfolio or small briefcase with paper to take notes.

- Extra copies of your resume.

six

□ □ □ □ □ □ □ □ □ □

15 Things You Should Never Do Once You Get a Job or in Your Career—Ever

If you have found your new position as you've been reading this book, let me be one of many to say: Hooray! Congratulations! Well done!

Even if you're still searching, this chapter is for you. Because you *will* find a new position. It's a matter of time and the right people, problems, and situation (with a little help from the stars and the moon) coming together. This chapter will help you be prepared for when that happens.

Here are the 15 things you should never do once you get a job or in your career—ever. Knowing these 15 things will make this next transition smooth and productive and your overall career more successful.

The 15 items are in the same format you've grown accustomed to—and, I hope, find helpful—listing not only the Don'ts, but also the Do's. And where I typically tell you what "Employers will conclude," I offer what "Others will conclude" when it makes sense. The "others" include your new manager, your company comrades, clients, customers, and anyone with whom you have contact in your job.

#1: Don't Disregard Those Who Helped You Get This Job and the Rest of the Jobs You'll Discover in Your Career

Connecting with others is in our genes. And it's probably how you found past jobs and discovered helpful information and other sources in your career. If you do it with care, it's how you'll find career positions in the future.

With so many people feeling swamped at work and overwhelmed with fear for their jobs, they forget this most basic principle of human nature: that we are built to connect with other people. And that people get something out of helping you, too.

Holistic physician and author Dr. Rick Kirschner says there's "a reciprocal instinct that if we do for others, the more likely they will do for us."

It's like a "caveman version of 'I scratch your back because I want you to scratch mine when I need it,'" explains psychotherapist Charles Allen.

It comes down to this: Careers thrive on relationships with live humans. Those relationships require attention.

MY 3 RULES ON HOW TO TREAT PEOPLE YOU CONNECT WITH IN YOUR CAREER

1. *Properly thank anyone who has shared their time and expertise.* It doesn't matter if they were directly or indirectly involved in helping you get your new job. Whether they made a call on your behalf or sat down and met with you for two hours. Or chatted by phone or e-mail or offered tepid advice.

Minimally, everyone gets a thank-you e-mail.

These people have invested their time in you. They are now part of your network. So when you get your new position, let them know how things turned out. Write them a personal note like this:

> Dear Belinda,
>
> I'm pleased to let you know that I have accepted the position of vice president of communications for the Baton Corporation, 3D Printer Manufacturing. The company converts digital files into three-dimensional objects and has incredible growth potential in health-care, architecture, and other industries.
>
> My responsibilities include the handling of daily communications with the media and the company's growing customer base, and I am thrilled to be a part of this new endeavor.
>
> Thank you so much for your support and encouragement while I was in the process of my job search. I especially appreciated your referral to Louis Lamotte, who helped me learn more about this growing industry. I wish you much success in the upcoming year and look forward to keeping in contact. Please let me know if I can help you in any way.
>
> Sincerely,

If you want to show your appreciation and be remembered forever by someone who was particularly generous and helpful, write and mail this person a note. Send a card. Send flowers, a gift card to Starbucks, a CD of their favorite music, or something else you know they'd like. Just thank them for being an incredible human being and helping you in your time of need.

2.   *Don't wait until you need something to keep in contact.* How rude is that? Very. I know you're busy. So is everyone else. Keeping in contact with people needs to be part of your busyness. Not an afterthought or something you do when your career is in trouble. Or when you need a reference or some information.

This business of relationship building is not about scheming maneuvers and machinations the likes of those in spy novels to get people to share their list of contacts. It's organic. It's like planting a seed. You have to keep watering.

Which means picking up the phone every once in a while and checking in with people you know, like, and want to help in return. It won't kill you to send an e-mail or text or just to say "Hello, I was thinking of you." Have lunch. Attend events that others invite you to that are near and dear to their hearts. Support them the way they've supported you.

3.   *Don't expect people who don't know you to drop everything to help you.* Some might. Most won't. But many will be more willing to connect if you've been referred by someone they know and trust.

Think about how it would be if you were in their shoes. You get an e-mail from a stranger named Adele Simpson. She says, "Your cousin Manny Shepowitz suggested I call you . . ." You trust Manny. He wouldn't sic anyone on you he didn't like and trust. So odds are pretty good you'll respond and set a time to talk to Adele. All because she was referred by your cousin Manny. It may take some time to get on your calendar. But now you're open to it.

Just as we instinctively know we need each other to survive in life, we need each other to thrive in our careers. Do what comes naturally. And do it regularly.

Don't

- Only contact people when you need something or your career is in trouble.

- Expect people who don't know you to help you.

- Scan the room at social or business events or walk away in the middle of a conversation to approach someone else you think is a "hot prospect."

- Expect people to help you if you never do anything in return.

- Forget to let your network of contacts know about your new job and to keep in contact.

Others will conclude . . .

- You don't care about the relationship—only about what you can get from them.

Do

- Plant seeds and seek out others with no gain in mind.

- Thank everyone who helps you—minimally by e-mail.

- Offer your assistance to others.

#2: Don't Act Like a Know-It-All

If you're brand new on the scene of a company, be all ears. Do a lot of listening and observing. Your way of doing things or ideas on what needs immediate attention might be spot-on. But take your time. Get to know the lay of the land. The people. The issues and the way folks conduct business. How things get done—or not. How people communicate. Do they rely on e-mail, or is sitting down to have a conversation the norm?

What are the most pressing issues they're facing? What are the broader and immediate goals?

If you don't lay low and observe for a while, people will resent it. They'll wonder, Just who do you think you are coming in here like a steam roller? They'll feel like you're trying to steal their thunder and make yourself look good at their expense. They'll think you have no appreciation for their efforts and what it took to get something done before you came on.

So when you feel the urge to intervene or make changes right away, resist.

If possible, during your first month or so at a new job get to work early and stay a little later. This will help you get a better feel for the place and how things run.

Depending on your team and type of work, sit down and meet the people you interact with. Ask lots of questions. Go to lunch and get to know them.

A woman named Gina told me that when she starts a new job she makes it a point "to know the security guard and cleaning crew. They know the ins and outs of the company and provide me with an impromptu 'New Employee Orientation.' They know everyone's schedules."

She adds that they sometimes even know "the company's strategic plan because the bigwigs talk freely around them because they are 'the help.'"

Sit down with your manager and make sure you're clear on what is expected of you, what your job priorities are, and how he or she likes to communicate, and how often.

Later, once you're acclimated and know the players, issues, and politics, you can offer more of your thoughts and opinions.

And after you've been with a company a while, be wary of not being open to hearing *others'* perspectives. Especially new folks. Remember, you were new and fresh once too.

Don't

- Intervene right away and immediately spout off your opinion on how things should be done.

- Tune out new ideas and differing ways of doing things.

Others will conclude . . .

- You don't care what they think.

- You don't respect their knowledge and expertise.

- You'll be difficult to work with.

- You're full of yourself.

Do

- More listening than talking.

- Get to know the people you work with—what they're like and how they think.

- When it's reasonable, listen to all sides before commenting.

- Learn your manager's priorities and how he or she likes to communicate.

- Show your appreciation and understanding for others' contributions.

#3: Don't Assume No One Is Paying Attention to You

An actor named Bob Elkins once told a meeting of budding filmmakers in Cincinnati to beware because "You're always auditioning." In other words, you may be making an impression on someone and not even know it, which can lead to an opportunity you weren't even thinking about. Or not. And I don't mean just online.

This is handy advice even if you're not an actor. One of my clients is an executive for a large company. Twice a month she sits around an intimidating conference table with 14 other executives to discuss strategic planning, investments, and other things executives discuss. She's the quiet type. She thinks great thoughts in her head, not out loud. Until a few weeks ago she didn't realize that she was auditioning for senior vice president of a new division. She didn't get the part.

"I was told I don't express my opinion enough, I'm too timid, and no one thinks I'm a strategic thinker. I didn't know I was being evaluated for something that didn't even exist yet."

You never know who's watching and when. One man who owns an advertising agency told me about the evening he was attending a local ad club awards show. He noticed a "guy who kept getting called up to accept awards. I didn't need anyone at the time, but made a mental note." Six months later, when he had an opening, he knew just who he wanted to talk to for the job.

People also pay attention to the individual in the room who asks tough questions. The kinds of questions that will push the company forward. They sit up and listen to the person who challenges assumptions. Who says, "Why not? What else? What more can we do? Why can't we do that? What can we do to remake this and push it to somewhere else?"

You may not get the job or promotion you want at the exact moment you'd like. Things rarely happen the way we think they will. But ideas and impressions are always percolating, and things happen in due time. So in the meantime, think about this:

- What are you doing to get noticed by people in your industry?

- What are you doing to make sure your good work is getting air time at your company?

- What are you doing to establish a good reputation within and outside your company?

- Are you asking questions that challenge the status quo?

As Elkins also says, "Good actors are artists who listen to what is and is not there." You may not be an actor. But if you have a career you'll want to be listening for what's not there—yet—and be aware of upcoming opportunities.

Don't

- Miss out on opportunities to speak up and offer your two cents.

- Think the only person who matters is your manager.

- Think the only people who matter are the ones you see every day at your company.

Others will conclude . . .

- You're not leadership material.

- You lack that "special something."

□ You don't have that much to contribute.

□ You're not a strategic thinker.

□ You don't have anything they need or want.

Do

□ Look for ways to be visible and active in your industry.

□ Look for ways to be visible and involved in your company.

□ Ask the tough questions. Challenge assumptions. Ask "Why not? What else? What more can we do? Why can't we do that?"

□ Remember that you're always auditioning for your next role.

#4: Don't Focus on Merely Being Employed

When you get a new job, the tendency is to 1) be relieved and 2) hope you can stay there as long as possible. And if it doesn't work out, you go back to wondering, *Where are the jobs?*

When you're focused on merely being employed, you're not thinking about what matters even more, both now and in the future—which is, how to keep yourself *employable*.

That means thinking about new ways you could apply your talents and interests as the world, your industry, and the company change.

Thinking like this means you're less likely to be in that constant state of asking, "Where's my next job?" or trying desperately to hold on to the job you've got.

Yes, this takes time. And yes, the work world will keep changing—probably mostly due to technology. But if you do your homework you'll stumble upon all kinds of enlightening discoveries. And that will lead you to a way to stay employable the rest of your career.

It's a matter of looking at trends and asking questions that focus on what work will be needed as a result of those trends.

Cynthia Wagner, editor of the *Futurist*, talks about three approaches to help you do that. They include "retrofitting," which means thinking about how you can add new skills to an existing job.

An example is the successful plumber referenced in a *New York Times Magazine* article (November 23, 2011) on the new economic rules, "who has mastered all the new water-flow sensor technology and pipe-fitting innovations . . . and can make more than $100,000 a year, while other plumbers who just know the basics, could make less than $20,000."

How do you "retrofit" your career now and in the future? Ask yourself these questions:

- How do technological trends and social changes apply to my career?

- What new skills and knowledge can I add to my line of work to support those?

- Can I incorporate new trends into my current work, and if so, how?

Wagner points to "blending careers."

This occurs when you make a connection between two or more separate areas. You can do this by combining skills or functions from different jobs or industries to create new specialties.

She cites the blending of work in human and environmental health. This has resulted in the emerging field of environmental health nursing, where professionals treat patients exposed to toxins.

A broader look at this field includes occupational and environmental health nursing.

One of my clients, who had 15 years of sales experience and a personal interest in Crohn's disease, is another example. He had developed exceptional skills as a persuasive communicator and excellent presenter. He *blended* these skills with his interest and became a medical educator specializing in Crohn's disease.

What skills, interests, and talents do you have that you can blend into a new specialty and fit a growing need?

The third approach is good old problem solving. To help you stay employable, look at problems people will face and come up with new roles and functions to help solve them.

For example, problems the communications age has brought on include privacy and security. As a result, one growing area is digital footprint management.

As issues like privacy, terrorism, and rage in society become more prominent, new problems will evolve around security in cyberspace, immigration, security preparedness, and food safety.

As trends develop and new problems arise, what services will be needed to support customers and businesses? Which ones interest you?

Once you get your new job, ask these questions soon—and often.

Don't

- Assume everything will go along as it is.

- Think your job will stay the same.

- Figure that you're safe and sound as long as you do a good job.

Do

- Sit down and think about the technological trends and social trends that affect your career and line of work and how you can "retrofit" your career.

- Consider what new skills and knowledge you can add to support these trends.

- Ask yourself what skills, interests, and talents you have that can blend into a new specialty and fit a growing need.

- Look at new problems that are arising and ask yourself: *What new services will be needed to support my customers and clients, and which ones interest me?*

#5: Don't Get Sloppy

Have you ever noticed that when you hire someone (it could be to clean your house or mow your lawn), they start out full of promise? But then something changes. They get sloppy.

They start showing up late. Sometimes completely forgetting to show up. "I've been busy" is a common excuse. They ignore e-mails. They begin to overlook details they were so good with at the beginning. They just don't seem to have the same level of conscientiousness or commitment.

Employers notice the same thing. And I am one of them.

I had just hired a young woman to help me with social media. She showed up for our first meeting. But by the second meeting, she had dropped the ball. We had scheduled it for a Saturday morning. At 7:30 the night before the meeting, she sent me an e-mail saying, "Would you mind if we rescheduled to another day? My weekend is shaping up. I'd like to do such-and-such instead." That was a short-lived relationship.

When Jillian Zavitz was programs manager for TalktoCanada. com, a company that provides online training in the English language, many of the new teachers she hired started out great, "signing into work early, responding to all of my e-mails, doing everything on time." Then, she says, "things started to slip-slop up."

They started arriving right on the hour (instead of ahead of time to prepare the class). They made up lame excuses. She says people took advantage of the swine flu, "calling in sick left, right, and center. They said their alarm didn't go off, they have a headache, took muscle relaxers. Why they accepted the job in the first place is beyond me."

What changes?

Is the good-worker-gone-bad syndrome due to a generation lacking a strong work ethic, as some say? It's not fair to make such a generalization.

Some people are just more conscientious than others. Folks who aren't especially conscientious may act conscientious about things at first—often because they need to pay close attention when learning a new job. But once they start doing the task over and over, things slide.

Psychologically speaking, to save energy the brain stops investing as much care into the job. Apparently the "low-on-conscientiousness" people don't value being prepared or careful in their work.

However, people who are conscientious will more likely be seen as doing a good job and will be more likely to get ahead.

If you don't become more conscientious you become more trouble than you're worth. Sometimes the company just "gets rid of the bad egg before they make everyone rotten," says Zavitz.

Or if you're a contract employee, they just never call you again.

Don't

▫ Start out gung ho and slack off once you know the drill.

▫ Make a commitment any less important than it was the moment you committed to it.

Others will conclude . . .

▫ You don't care about the work.

▫ You're not detail-oriented.

▫ You don't really want the job.

▫ They can't count on you.

Do

▫ Connect conscientious performance to achievement.

▫ Check your work more carefully.

▫ Make a conscious decision to stick with a project longer than you normally would.

▫ Stick to your commitments.

#6: Don't Assume You Know Everything You Need to Know

If you're going to get this next job and flourish in your field or in a new one, your success will boil down to living with this question: How will I ward off irrelevance?

The answer is to continually think about how to *stay* relevant. How to have the *knowledge, skills,* and *mindset* that will help your employer, or a new one, to be successful, help keep customers happy, and entice new ones. You do that by making *self-development* a priority.

Peter Drucker, hailed as the father of modern management, was one of the most influential business and social thinkers of our time, inspiring the likes of Tom Peters, Jack Welch, and Andrew Grove. In his book, *A Class with Drucker* (AMACOM, 2007), William Cohen explains that Drucker employed four main vehicles for self-development. They were *reading, writing, listening,* and *teaching.*

So here's what you should be asking yourself:

- What do I need to *read* and *research* to help my company or a new one evolve? What do I need to learn to help it constantly make progress? What do I need to learn to enrich my own skills?

- What should I *write* to clarify my own ideas or influence others to help us stay competitive?

- Who do I need to be *meeting* with and *listening* to to deepen my insight so I can help my company or another stay competitive?

- What can I *teach* to help form my ideas and clarify my own thinking?

As Cohen points out, Drucker told his own students, "The best way to learn is to teach" and that "I teach to find out what I think."

Living with the question of how you will ward off irrelevance helps your career live long and prosper. And while you're at it, leave your competition in the dust.

Don't

- Stop reading, researching, and seeking new ideas.

Others will conclude . . .

- You're not aware of the latest trends and ideas.

- You can't help them stay competitive and evolve.

Do

- Ward off irrelevance.

- Enrich your skills.

- Write to clarify your ideas.

- Meet with and listen to others to help you deepen your insight.

- Teach to help form your ideas.

#7: Don't Forget to Track Your Accomplishments

Remember the first thing we talked about in Chapter 4: Don't Talk About Things You Can't Back Up? And how, in order for an employer to see your value, you need to make your claims come to life?

Next, I said you needed to come up with your "proof." Specific examples that help employers see you are the solution to their problems. Proof that makes them say, "OK, I see how you did that in the past. That's what I want you to do for me."

If you have been good at tracking your accomplishments, that exercise shouldn't have been too difficult. But if you haven't been doing a good job of that, you've got homework to do. And it doesn't stop once you find your next position.

You want to continue to track your accomplishments because:

- You never know when you'll be looking for a new job. Things can change on a dime. Being in a new role, you'll have new "proof" to share. If you don't track it, you'll forget it when you need it.

- You'll want to add examples of what you're accomplishing in your new role to your resume. If you track your accomplishments, you've got the information handy when you need it.

- You need to keep your boss informed of all the great work you're doing. That would include things you're working on and accomplishments you've achieved. If you don't track these, your work will blur together. You'll forget the specifics. But if you track it, come performance review time, you'll make it a lot easier on yourself.

Tracking this information doesn't have to be complicated. Designate a notebook, folder, or a place on your computer or other electronic device where you capture your accomplishments as they happen. All you have to write is something like this:

> "May 20: Within first two weeks on job, gave two-hour presentation to senior management, entire hair care division, and marketing department that set the new global strategy. Everyone loved it." (In six months, hopefully you can add to this by describing the great results the strategy achieved.)

Don't

- Wait until your performance review or when you need an updated resume to think about how you're adding value.

Do

- Get into the habit of once a week or so asking yourself, What did I accomplish this week?—and then writing it down in your special folder.

#8: Don't Count on Anyone to Watch Over Your Career

Even if you have a mentor or coach who is sworn to advise you every step of the way or a supervisor who's a big believer in career planning, don't count on it. Have you noticed they're just as swamped and stressed out as you?

Cultivate a new habit that will keep your career as safe and secure as a career can get these days: the "Keep a Watch Over Yourself" habit.

It is based on the fact that everyone else is too busy with their own problems to worry about your career.

The issue of where you're headed and how you'll get there is your baby. The only way to make sure you are getting where you want is by keeping a watch over yourself.

Buy a "Watch Over Me Notebook" (or create a folder on your computer) that will be used for this purpose only.

You'll focus on two main areas. First, yourself.

At home or whenever you can schedule 10 minutes of quiet, alone time, answer these five questions related to you:

1. What am I working toward? Do I have a particular goal, level of expertise, or title that I've set my sights on?

2. To help me get there, what do I still need to learn? What do I lack to become totally competent at what I do now—and to move to the next level?

3. What do I need to master so I feel confident I am the best

I can be? Are there certain techniques or skills I need in order to progress?

4. What experiences, training, exposure, or type of thinking would help me achieve what I just wrote?

5. Now, what am I going to do to make this happen?

Schedule a meeting with yourself for one month from the date you answered these questions. At that meeting, ask yourself, *Did I do what I said I needed to do to progress?* Then schedule a meeting with yourself a month from then to check in again. Do this every month.

The second area is similar to what I discussed in #6 about staying relevant and employable. Track that information (the questions I told you to ask yourself in #6) and use it as your guide. Remember, you can't rest on your laurels.

So the second way you'll keep a watch over yourself is to stay clued in to a broader view of what's happening in the world in general and your industry in particular.

Besides reading reputable industry news, keeping up with world news, and talking to people to learn what's on their minds—and jotting down ideas—answer these questions in your dedicated notebook or file:

- How will my work be affected by economic changes and such trends as population growth, longer life spans, loss of traditional culture, and decline of the environment?

- What problems have I learned about that could affect my field but no one is doing anything about and will probably get bigger?

- How will my profession be affected by technology?

- Keeping these problems, changes, and trends in mind, what

can I do to enhance my value to my employer or clients? What do I need to learn more about or do to stay current?

Make an appointment with yourself in six months to revisit these questions. Ask yourself, *Did I do what I said I would? What else has changed?*

Don't

▫ Assume a mentor, coach, or manager is watching out for your career.

Do

▫ Think through and write down in a designated place what you're working toward and how you'll get there.

▫ Schedule meetings with yourself to check on your progress.

▫ Track economic changes and trends that affect your work and what you can do about them that makes you more valuable to your company.

#9: Don't Ignore Your Own and Others' Feelings

When people come to work each day, they don't leave their personal problems, insecurities, and personality quirks at home. They come marching right into the office with them. That's one reason there are so many conflicts, annoying people, and situations in which you can easily lose your cool.

There are hundreds of things that can pull you off your center in a day. With so much close interaction between you, customers, peers, and bosses, emotions can run high. Many jobs are lost and careers derailed because of the way people act with each other, respond to stress, or deal with a conflict.

It often comes down to this: people don't understand how they come across. They don't notice that they get swept away by their emotions. They don't recognize the feelings of others. Some of the smartest people don't get this. You can be supersmart when it comes to IQ and not so smart in the area of emotional intelligence.

The subject of emotional intelligence has been researched, studied and discussed for years. Daniel Goleman, author of *Emotional Intelligence: Why It Can Matter More than IQ* (Bantam Books, 1995), focuses on the essential human competencies of emotional intelligence such as "self-awareness, self-control and empathy, and the arts of listening, resolving conflicts and cooperation."

This concept has been covered in *Time* magazine, on *20/20*, and on *Oprah*. Yet many people still confuse emotional intelligence with simply "being nice."

I hear a lot of people insist they have no time to pay attention to what they are feeling, let alone feelings of others. But you know what? Emotions can't be stopped—even when you're at work.

Without getting into the science, Goleman points out two minds—the emotional and the rational—that operate in tight harmony to guide us through the world. But "when passions surge the balance tips," he says, and it's the emotional mind that captures the upper hand.

The Other Kind of Smart (AMACOM, 2009), by Harvey Deutschendorf, defines emotional intelligence as "an array of attributes and tools that enable us to deal with the pressure and demands of our environment." It's like an "advanced common sense," he says.

Testing shows that 27 to 45 percent of success on the job is determined by our emotional intelligence, he says.

You can increase yours. Start by learning more about what it is. Practice new approaches with people.

Part of emotional intelligence is having empathy. That is noticing and acknowledging others' feelings. This ability allows you "to see the situation that the person is in, yet step back and act in a manner that would ultimately be in that person's best interest," says Deutschendorf.

If that doesn't come naturally to you, try this suggestion from Deutschendorf. First, observe a group of people having a conversation that you're not directly involved in. Then try to figure out how each person is feeling by noticing tone of voice, facial expressions, and words with underlying meanings.

Some of the most valued employees I've worked with are the ones with high "EQ" (emotional quotient). They trust themselves to say the right words or take the best action when they're in the thick of things. They have the wherewithal to approach exasperating conversations with sensitivity. They can get their point across *and* save the relationship.

The smartest workers know that even with all the high-tech ways we conduct business, it still involves high-touch interactions with living, breathing humans.

Don't

- Underestimate the importance of how you come across.

- Ignore the feelings of others.

- Ignore your own feelings.

Others will conclude . . .

- You are difficult to get along with.

- You don't care about anything or anyone but yourself.

- You don't care about people, period.

Do

▫ Pay attention to what you feel.

▫ Develop an awareness for how others feel. Observe others—notice their tone of voice, expressions, and what their words aren't saying.

▫ Develop the ability to step back and see what's in the other person's interest.

▫ Pay close attention to how you come across and how people react to you.

#10: Don't Insist on Knowing How Things Will Turn Out

You're in a new job and if all goes well, you'll be happy, do great work, and be there for a good spell. Of course no one knows for sure how things will turn out. No one can predict with certainty how your company and industry will fare. These days there are just too many uncertainties.

So how do you plan for your future when you don't know what's around the corner?

One thing we do know is that the pace of change is accelerating due to "exponential growth of information technology," says Ray Kurzweil, a speaker I heard at the WorldFuture 2010 conference and interviewed for my column.

Dubbed by *Inc.* magazine as the "rightful heir to Thomas Edison," this inventor and author demonstrates just how quickly change is occurring.

"The first steps in technology—fire, stone tools, the wheel—took tens of thousands of years to take hold," Kurzweil says. "Gutenberg's invention of the printing press took about 400 years to reach a mass audience. The telephone reached a quarter of the U.S. population in 50 years, the cell phone did that in seven years. Social networks, wikis, and blogs took about three years."

A tool of choice for thinking about today and your future and making decisions in the midst of uncertainty is called *scenario planning*. The military began using it after World War II to imagine what enemies might do and to plan alternative strategies.

It's been used extensively by Shell Oil, which in the 1970s was looking for events that might affect the price of oil.

Scenario thinking is an organized way to "dream effectively about our own future," Kurzweil says. It helps you present "alternative images of the future, not just extrapolating the trends of the present" and make choices today with an understanding of how they might turn out.

It forces you to not just ask questions like this one: What are the driving forces—economic, political, technological, legal, and societal—affecting my industry and career? But also these: What's uncertain and what's predictable? What could happen based on that uncertainty or predictability? What if that didn't happen? How would that rock my industry or career?

Scenario planning can help you rehearse how you respond to possible futures and spot early warning signs as they unfold, said Lawrence Wilkinson, cofounder of the think tank Global Business Network, in *Wired* (2009).

Thinking like this helps you be more creative about your future and how to get there. It helps you anticipate and be better prepared for changes by considering consequences, risks, and opportunities and coming up with plausible alternatives.

Not thinking like this can put you "at a loss for ways to act when upheaval continues," says Peter Schwartz, author of *The Art of the Long View* (Currency Doubleday, 1996).

And not thinking like this may also make you seem unwilling

to take risks. This kind of thinking takes discipline and the hardest thing of all: to stop insisting to know exactly how things will turn out. Because as the futurists are so fond of saying, no one knows for sure.

Don't

- Be focused on making the perfect "right" choice.

- Think you can research away the uncertainties.

Others will conclude . . .

- You're unwilling to try new things and make mistakes.

- You're a control freak.

Do

- Brainstorm and dream effectively about your future. Do scenario planning by coming up with alternative images of the future.

- Spot early warning signs.

- Anticipate and be prepared for changes by considering consequences, risks, and opportunities.

- Consider what could rock your industry or career.

- Make choices with an understanding of how they might turn out.

- Come up with plausible alternatives.

- Prepare to respond to the "what ifs."

#11: Don't Let Your Soul Get Sucked Dry

You know what people complain about most when it comes to their work? That all that time they spend at work is just downright unfulfilling.

They run from one deadline to the next, reacting to e-mails and instant messages and checking things off their to-do list. They want to know, "How can I have more meaning in what I do?"

For some people, it's a matter of completely changing the type of work they do. Asking big questions like, *How do I want to spend my time? Who do I want to spend it with? What do I want to create or who do I want to serve?* These are good questions to visit from time to time.

It's also wise to evaluate how things are going at your job from time to time by asking yourself, *Am I using my best skills? Am I still enjoying this work? How do I want to grow and develop in this job and with this company?*

But sometimes, more fulfillment can come about just by choosing to have a purpose for the work you do—not just goals.

I understand that your company sets goals and metrics and that they are necessary for success. But as IMPAQ CEO Mark Samuel says in his book *Making Yourself Indispensable: The Power of Personal Accountability* (Portfolio, 2012), "Goals without a purpose behind them will generally create an 'empty' feeling of going through the motions."

But making the choice between being purpose-driven or goal-driven "has the highest correlation to success, indispensability and personal fulfillment."

Whether your company sets goals to achieve customer satisfaction, sales, or quality, "It becomes about being busy and doing what we are told rather than about making a meaningful difference," he says. There's no clear sense of purpose.

But if you are purpose-driven, you are dedicated. And "in that dedication you will go beyond satisfactory performance or acceptable communication to achieve excellent results."

So for instance, if you decide your purpose is to have satisfied customers, it's not your checklist that is most important. "It will be your care, concern and dedication to serving your customer that drives your communication, behavior and actions. You will go out of your way to serve your customer because that is your purpose," Samuel says. And that adds up to more personal fulfillment and appreciation.

Don't

- Forget to stop and evaluate how things are going with your work.

- Just meet goals.

- Just check off your daily to-do list.

Do

- Choose to be purpose-driven.

- Stop from time to time and ask yourself the "big" questions about whether you're doing what you want to do.

#12: Don't Leave in a Huff

There are many reasons to call it quits at a job. You may only have been in your new position a few months, but it's clear—this is not where you want to be.

It could be years before the honeymoon is over. You just know that it's time to move on. The work has become boring. Or your daily duties are simply intolerable. You and your boss don't see eye-to-eye and never will. The company's culture is a major misfit. The list goes on.

But when it's quitting time, there are few good reasons to walk out in a huff with no explanation. Or to wave ta-ta at the end of the day, then e-mail your resignation with no plan to return. It's the chicken way out.

It's also the wrong thing to do for many reasons. For one thing, this is your reputation you're putting on the line. Word will get out. People know where you used to work and they know people who work there. If you're suddenly not there one day, people will talk.

When your former manager and potential employer in the same industry talk (for the sake of this argument we'll say they know each other), the conversation may go something like this:

> **Potential new boss:** "Lucy Laburbaton just contacted us about work. What happened?"
>
> **Former boss:** "It was weird. She left work on Tuesday and the next morning she e-mailed her resignation. She had been to the office in the middle of the night and cleaned out her stuff and took our information off her computer."

How do you think that makes you *seem*? Certainly not very professional. The fact that you resigned by e-mail without a word to your employer is bad enough. Coming into the office when it's closed and taking proprietary information is another issue—and something you should never do.

Both behaviors bring up all kinds of questions about your maturity, critical thinking skills, integrity, and ability to communicate and work well with others.

You've also just scorched a relationship with your former boss— and people who know him or her. Which could be a lot. Did you know that researchers now say the average number of acquaintances separating any two people in the world is 4.74?

The point is, it's a small world. News spreads fast these days. And that can affect your chances of getting a new job.

Some people leave their jobs in a more vocal huff. You may recall Greg Smith, who wrote an op-ed article in the *New York Times* March 14, 2012 (and seven months later, a book), about why he left Goldman Sachs. And how can you forget the Jet-Blue flight attendant who resigned his job in 2010 in what was described as a profanity-laced public announcement that ended with the words "I've had it," and then grabbed some beers, deployed the airplane's emergency escape chute, and slid down onto the tarmac.

If you ever find yourself at such an emotional crossroad, think about what you're trying to accomplish before you light that bridge-burning match. Must you tell your company and others what you really think? Where does it get you? Leaving your job like a drama queen rarely works.

If things aren't working out—and depending on the issue and circumstances—a conversation with your manager could be in order to see if the situation is fixable. But if it's time to leave, fine. Just do it in a way that doesn't put your coworkers and manager in a tight spot by leaving with no warning. And leave in a way that protects your reputation.

Yes, this is a difficult conversation to hold. But it's necessary and doable. Do it behind closed doors. In person is best. And use your indoor voice.

Explain your intention to leave and your appreciation for the opportunity you've had. Don't dwell on negatives. Keep it brief and offer to help make it a smooth transition.

Follow up with a letter stating your intention to leave, the date your resignation is effective, and again, a few words about your appreciation for the opportunity you've had.

Doing the right thing will make it less awkward and difficult when you're interviewing for your next job. But even if you have already found your next job, it's best to leave on a good note. You still have to live with the story that will follow you around. Venting your frustrations privately can be therapeutic. But doing so in public or without an explanation can be catastrophic. It may be harder to do the right thing. But it may be much easier on your career, overall.

Don't

- Leave your job in an "I quit!" huff.

- Write resignation letters that go into all kinds of negative details about why you're leaving.

- Turn your resignation into a public spectacle.

- Resign by e-mail and never come back.

Others will conclude . . .

- You're immature and unprofessional.

- You lack integrity.

- You're a lousy communicator.

- You don't handle uncomfortable situations well.

Do

- Hold a private conversation with your manager about your intention. Stick to facts. Offer to help with the transition.

#13: Don't Do Your Work for Anyone but Yourself

Someone once told me—it may have been my husband, who tells me lots of wise things—that when writing, write for yourself first. Be your first audience, he said. If you don't enjoy what you wrote, don't like it, or don't think it's any good, neither will anyone else.

I love this advice. I remember it every time I sit down to write my column or a sentence in a book. It helps me do my best work and enjoy it.

I think this applies to any kind of work. You should be your first audience—no matter what you do. I don't care if you're stacking shelves or preparing a report for the chairman of the board. Do it according to the high standards you set for yourself in everything you do.

If you're writing your resume, write it for yourself first. It should be brimming with information that describes you the way you want to be seen. Remember the "How I Want to Be Remembered After I Leave the Room" Exercise and your "How I Want to Be Seen" Profile (both in Chapter 2)? Sure, keep in mind everything we talked about earlier. Think of the audience of potential employers you're writing it for. Make sure your resume is accurate and void of exaggeration. But write it according to *your* standards first. Make sure it conveys the message you want so that you can say to yourself, *This is the best piece of work I could create. I feel good about it.*

Of course your manager, manager's boss, coworkers, clients, readers, viewers—whomever is the recipient of your dedicated efforts—will be delighted when you do your best work. That will be the natural outcome if you are your first audience.

Don't

- Do work just to please others.

Do

- Be your first audience.

- Do work that you feel good about and meets your standards.

#14: Don't Get Careless with Your Online Presence

First, don't forget to update your information now that you landed a new position. Up until now, for example, your LinkedIn profile has been crafted as one for a job hunter. So consider unchecking (under "Opportunity Preferences") the box that indicates you're interested in Job Inquiries. (I know people who have gotten fired when their managers found out or thought they were looking for a new job.)

Update your summary and experience. You're no longer a real estate agent looking for work. You're now associated with Mark and Mandy's Real Estate, where you help property owners in the tri-state area sell their homes faster and for a higher price. Write something like that in your profile.

And now that you may be trying to attract clients to your business, be strategic about what you say. Rather than just listing your title as "Economist," for example, look back at some of the wording you used in your "How I Want to Be Seen" Profile. How about a version of this: "Economist who solves complex economic programs related to profitability, modeling, and forecasting for my clients."

Don't be a "gimme, gimme" networker, says Krista Canfield, corporate communications manager at LinkedIn. That's someone who's always asking for help, contacts, and information, but doesn't help others.

Look for ways to bond with others. Review the status updates LinkedIn sends you that tell you when someone has received a promotion or gotten a new client. Congratulate those folks.

Look for interesting people to meet. Join and participate in groups. Answer questions people post.

The same guidelines apply that we talked about in Chapter 4 under #15: Don't contact potential clients or others and lie about your relationship. Don't say you know them when you don't. If you want to meet someone, again, the best approach is to ask for an introduction through someone you know. If you write to a person directly, personalize your note.

And now that you work for a new company, don't exaggerate or misrepresent your work or what the company does.

Use a photo in your profile. It builds a level of trust and familiarity when someone can see your face. And if you're meeting a new potential client for coffee, knowing what you look like makes it easier for them to find you. Keep it professional, using a head shot you own. I know of job hunters who used the photograph their former company took for public relations purposes or internal use. That photo usually belongs to your former employer. If you're thinking of using it, ask permission first.

Also, unless you're a yoga instructor, don't post a photo of yourself sitting in a one-legged King Pigeon yoga pose.

And remember, you now represent a company or some other entity. Everything you say is a reflection of the company and the way it does business.

So be careful what you post on Facebook and Twitter. Take the case of Jay Townsend, a campaign adviser to New York Representative Nan Hayworth. On May 26, 2012, he posted a comment on Facebook urging people to "hurl some acid" at Democratic female lawmakers he didn't agree with. He ended up resigning a week later. But when the controversy didn't die down, he apologized on Facebook saying:

"I posted a stupid, thoughtless, and insensitive comment on a Facebook page." He added: "The mistake was mine and mine only, and the post in no way was intended to represent the views of anyone for whom I have worked or represented."

But it *does* reflect on them. And that's how they'll see it.

Before you post anything online, think about this: Is it stupid, thoughtless, and insensitive? How will this affect my company? How could this be interpreted by strangers?

Don't forget that anything you write—e-mails included—can easily be sent and read by *anyone*. Think about what you're saying and how easy it would be for others to read it before you post or send off your opinions and comments.

I see all kinds of conversations on e-mail and Facebook that have no place there. These are comments made about sensitive issues or when emotions are running high and can easily be misunderstood. There are just some things that you need to pick up the phone and talk to someone about.

Online or not, always consider how a choice of words or actions can affect your career overall. The photographer Eve Arnold exemplifies this beautifully.

Arnold, who died at age 99, was "acclaimed for capturing celebrities in intimate moments after winning their trust," according to the obituary written by the *New York Times* (January 5, 2012).

It told of the time the actress Joan Crawford hired Arnold to take photos to promote her new movie. When Crawford arrived for the photo shoot, she was inebriated and demanded to be photographed naked. Arnold, who at first demurred, took the pictures. But a few days later she gave Crawford the negatives, assuring her they'd never be published.

Arnold told London newspaper the *Independent* that she "had never been tempted to make the nude photos public, not so much out of concern for Ms. Crawford's image as for her own."

"I didn't think they would do me credit," she said. "I had in mind a long career."

Don't

- Use the same profile information that positioned you as a job hunter.

- Contact potential clients and other contacts via LinkedIn and say "You know me" when they don't.

- Stretch the truth or lie about your credentials or your company.

- Be a gimme, gimme networker.

- Post stupid, thoughtless, and insensitive comments.

Others will conclude . . .

- You're dishonest.

- You lack integrity.

- You can't be trusted.

- You're thoughtless and insensitive.

- You only care about yourself.

Do

- Update your online profiles to reflect your current status. Use language that's strategic and positions you the way you want to be seen—as a professional at this company who can help potential clients or customers.

- Ask for introductions to people you don't know through people you do know or send personalized messages through LinkedIn's InMail feature.

- Consider how the material you post will affect your employer.

- Look for ways to bond with and support others.

#15: Don't Forget Who Brought You to the Dance

There are people you will meet throughout your career—not just in this job hunt—who are the special ones.

They help you beyond words, in ways you never knew you would need support, and in ways that make you deliriously successful.

It may happen when you are just starting out. Someone helps you get your first customer or client. It may be a mentor or a colleague who sticks with you through thick and thin. Someone who gives you a chance of a lifetime when no one else would give you the time of day. A client who introduces you to new opportunities that double your business.

Remember their good deeds. In fact, make sure they get preferential treatment.

That means, first of all, never forgetting what they did for you. It means never doing something that would harm that relationship. Even if it would benefit your career or business.

A man named James, who owns a small marketing company, told me of an incredible business opportunity he got because someone (we'll call him Don) brought him in on the ground floor of a big project. James was technically working for Don, since it was Don's client. But James did such a great job that the owners of the new business went behind Don's back and told James they'd pay him more if he dumped Don and worked for them directly.

James refused. He was beholden to Don, who had introduced him to this opportunity. He did not forget who brought him to the dance.

Don't

□ Betray the people who have helped you succeed.

□ Put relationships at risk.

□ Forget who helped you get ahead.

Others will conclude . . .

□ You lack integrity.

□ Your moral character is in question.

□ You can't be trusted.

□ You only care about yourself.

Do

□ Treat others the way you want to be treated.

□ Treat the people who have helped you with extra special care.

□ Remember who came to your rescue.

Other Don'ts to Help You in Your Career

□ *Don't burn bridges.* Just as we discussed in Chapter 4, it's best not to talk badly about past employers, clients, and coworkers—ever. You never know when you will run into them again later in your career.

□ *Don't assume your boss knows what you're working on and how well you're doing.* Everyone—including your manager—is busy with their own problems. Take the initiative to keep him or her updated. Reach out and ask for meetings or to sit down and do a quick update. Discussions about your performance don't have to be relegated to once or twice a year at official performance reviews.

▫ *Don't lie.* This never turns out well. Don't do it—ever.

▫ *Don't ignore people who reach out to you.* You know the feeling of sitting there waiting and wondering when, if ever, someone is going to return your call or respond to your e-mail. It's maddening. So don't do it to other people.

▫ *Don't be late.* People will resent you for making them sit there and wait for you to get to a meeting. Their time is just as important as yours. Set appointments and be there when you say you'll be there. It's that simple.

▫ *Don't assume companies just give promotions and raises.* Companies appreciate people who are valuable and do things to increase that value. So first, know how to do your job better than anybody. Make sure you focus on the tasks that help your company succeed.

Build a reputation for being helpful and supporting others. Volunteer to help. Offer to take on work that doesn't fit your job description or goes beyond the call of duty. When the time is right, make your case. Show how you've increased your value and earned a promotion or raise.

Getting things done is not good enough. Someone once said, "That which gets done can be measured." But that which gets done well can be measured and rewarded.

Conclusion

□ □ □ □ □ □ □ □ □ □

How to Make It in This Wild. and Crazy Time

I cannot recall a time in the last three-and-a-half decades when somebody, somewhere, was not feeling distressed about his or her career, ability to get work, and overall financial well-being.

Umpteen events have affected that. The oil crisis that started in the early 1970s. The savings and loan crisis that took place in the 1980s and early 1990s. Slow economic growth. Soaring inflation. Stagflation. Recessions. Illegal and unethical business practices. The information technology revolution. The 2000 burst of the dot-com bubble and the most recent financial crisis, which began in late 2007. Or something that had nothing to do with any of that.

If it's not been one thing, it's been another. It's always going to be that way. Times are generally wild and crazy. Just like it feels now. Perhaps this could be one of the most difficult times yet.

There is only one way through this particular wild and crazy time: Keep your head held high, focus on the outcomes you can affect, turn your values into habits, then hit employers with your best shot.

Please do not do this: Walk around complaining that it's the worst of times and no one is hiring. Instead do this. Ask yourself, *Have I done everything in my power to change, adapt, stay relevant, and then prepare for an employer's white-hot light of scrutiny?*

Most everything I've talked about here comes down to something I once heard Kofi Annan, former Secretary General of the United Nations, say: "Character trumps everything."

So perhaps most important, keep this in mind: A successful career is not about *what* you know or *who* you know. It's about *how you are*.

So be you. Be the best of you. And be well.

Acknowledgments

Even though writing a book entails mostly sitting here at my desk with my faithful and beloved black Labrador/Golden retriever mix rescue dog tangled up in my feet, I am hardly alone in this endeavor.

This book in particular—due to the timing, which coincided with my husband's scary health issues, surgery, and months of recuperation, all beginning during the week I planned to start writing—calls for special thanks.

First, to everyone who helped me when I asked for input, I am grateful. To all of the employers who shared their valuable insights. And to organizations like the Society for Human Resource Management, CareerBuilder, Google, and LinkedIn for your input. I especially appreciate the time Eric Zuckerman, Rob Basso, Dianne Durkin, Alex Churchill, Michael Zwick, Allan Young, and Bill Strauss took to answer my endless questions. And my thanks to Barb King, Trisha Bath, Nick Paddock, and Michelle Sullivan for your stories.

No project would be complete without the expert eyeballs of Randy McNutt, Cheryl Bauer, and Margaret McGurk.

Thank you to my editor, Ellen Kadin, at AMACOM, and my agent, Linda Konner, for believing in the book.

My deepest gratitude to Payton Baker, Michael and Beverly O'Brien, Diana Tayler, Bill and Nina Strauss, Brenda and Sterling Staggs, Dennis Rutherford, Mark Lutwak and Y York, Steve and Mary Anne Williams, B.J. Gray, Karen and Eddie Saeks, and other friends who brought nourishment, dragged in the garbage cans, or did dog walks the first three difficult months of 2012.

To my mother, my biggest cheerleader. And to Florence Kaufman, one of my other cheerleaders, who died this year and whose support I miss terribly.

Thank you to my husband, Greg Newberry, who is kind, strong, creative, and patient.

Thank you, dear reader. If it weren't for you, I wouldn't know who to talk to.

Index

About the Author

Andrea Kay is a career consultant, syndicated columnist, and author of six career books, including the popular book, *Life's a Bitch and Then You Change Careers: 9 Steps to Get Out of Your Funk and On to Your Future*. She specializes in "Career Therapy," in which she quickly gets to the heart of the issue to help people get where they want to go.

A weekly newspaper columnist since 1988, Andrea has written more than 1,300 articles on careers and workplace issues. Today, her syndicated column, "At Work," appears in *USA Today* and Gannett newspapers across the United States, other Gannett media, and on the web.

Andrea has been awarded the Women In Communications Gem Award for adherence to the highest standards of practice in professional communications and support of women in the workforce. She has been named Best Career Consultant as well as Leading Consultant and Trainer by Leading Women, and her books have been recognized for literary and artistic achievement.

Andrea is a volunteer mentor for the Writers Guild of America, East Foundation's Veterans Project, a writing workshop for veterans, and is an artist trying to help those dealing with Alzheimer's (FlutterbybyAndreaKay.com). She has also been learning Spanish for more than 20 years.

AndreaKay.com
http://www.linkedin.com/in/kayandrea
http://twitter.com/andreakaycareer